Coming
Back

Also by Fawn Germer

Work-Life Reset
Pearls
The Ah-Hah! Moment
Finding the Up in the Downturn
The New Woman Rules
Mermaid Mambo
Mustang Sallies
Hard Won Wisdom

To you. Yeah, I mean *you*. I know this seems daunting, but rise again. What if your greatest success hasn't even happened yet?

Coming Back

How to Win
the Job You Want
When You've Lost
the Job You Need

Fawn Germer

ST. MARTIN'S PRESS
NEW YORK

First published in the United States by St. Martin's Press, an imprint of St. Martin's Publishing Group

www.stmartins.com

Designed By Devan Norman

Library of Congress Cataloging-in-Publication Data

Names: Germer, Fawn, author.
Title: Coming back : how to win the job you want when you've lost the job you need / Fawn Germer.
Description: First edition. | New York : St. Martin's Press, [2020] | Includes index.
Identifiers: LCCN 2020040181 | ISBN 9781250271655 (hardcover) | ISBN 9781250271662 (ebook)
Subjects: LCSH: Career development. | Mid-career. | Career changes. | Job hunting.
Classification: LCC HF5381 .G4859 2020 | DDC 650.14—dc23
LC record available at https://lccn.loc.gov/2020040181

First Edition: 2021

10 9 8 7 6 5 4 3 2 1

Contents

Don't judge yourself by who you were
when things came easily.

Judge yourself by who you became
when things got tough.

Never, ever quit.

Introduction

Well, this kinda blows.

Work your ass off and then what? You feel like you are at the very top of your game, but you are being treated like crap or you can't get hired.

My guess is that you picked up this book because something isn't quite right. Either you have stalled out at work or you are having trouble getting the career opportunities you want (and deserve). Maybe you have lost your job, or left it to care for children, parents, or a loved one who needs help. Or you are among the millions of people fired, furloughed, reduced to part-time, or working at home and having to learn on the fly due to COVID-19 and its short- and longer-term impact. Maybe you have been forced to reinvent yourself, or maybe you are choosing to do it because, well, it's time.

Several years ago, I noticed an increasing number of emails from people who had seen me speak and wanted to know why, despite long, successful careers, they suddenly hit the wall. They felt disrespected and unwanted. Many were sure they were being discriminated against.

Suddenly, my usual positive message of using the Law of Attraction (you manifest what you think) to create your greatest success was falling flat. There was no way to repeat affirmations and wind up back on the fast track.

This situation required serious work.

After a leadership conference in Orlando, I went for drinks with several of the nation's top corporate heavyweights from the executive board. I was shocked when, as the liquor started to flow, they shared their career struggles as the corporate brass prepared to push them out. Their stories were the same as those of the people who'd been writing me, and the same stories I heard from my friends and neighbors.

What the hell?

I assumed the issue was age. How could it be anything else? So I started this project to focus on how to get seasoned professionals back on track in a workplace that, in many cases, has devalued their brilliance.

But it's not just age, and it's not just happening to middle-aged or older people.

The issue is relevance. You may be brilliant, but you may not be relevant. You may be experienced, but you may not be relevant. And the one thing you absolutely must be to make it today is RELEVANT. It is an issue if you are over forty and it is an issue if you are in your twenties.

My editor, George Witte, wisely realized that the obstacles faced by seasoned professionals are similar to those faced by others trying to return to work after taking extended time-outs to raise their babies, care for loved ones, deal with medical leaves, get more education, or travel the world. This book also speaks to you.

I have interviewed more than three hundred people for this book. Do you know the most surprising thing I found? That everybody is so shocked that these slaps in the face happen to *them*. They don't see it coming and they think they are exempt. They think they get a pass.

If you are in denial and think this isn't going to happen to you, or if you think, "You don't know my track record," then you need to keep reading very closely. It happens to the best of us. The people you look up to. The people you assume wouldn't have to worry about a thing.

If you are feeling discouraged, hang in there. I'm here to help. This book is designed to move you into action, taking the sometimes uncomfortable steps that will make you a viable, hirable professional once again.

Some thoughts to begin with:

There is no resting on laurels or skating. Jobs that allowed skating were eliminated years ago. We must constantly prove ourselves in a constantly changing world.

We are witnessing the death of experience. Many, many companies want innovative thinkers and big communicators who are ahead of the curve. They don't care about seniority and aren't all that interested in what you've done in the past.

It no longer matters whether you are the best person for the job today. What matters is where you are on the runway to deliver tomorrow and in five years.

If you learn about future trends from people at work, or rely on others to do things for you, you aren't taking responsibility for your own relevance. You must study how artificial intelligence, robotics, big data, machine learning, and blockchain could impact your work.

Success grows when you continue adding new skills. Fortunately, it is easy to learn and grow with online learning, and most of these opportunities cost very little or are free.

It's time to stop networking like a wimp.

If you want to be seen as current, you have to dress current.

If you are unwilling to do all of these things, find a company that is slow to change. They still exist. Somewhere. But ask yourself, will such a company last in this climate of change and upheaval?

So many people don't just need to work financially, they *want* to work—and can't get the opportunities they desire. They apply for dozens, hundreds, even thousands of jobs but rarely land interviews and haven't found anything that pays what they believe they deserve. They shared with me their feelings of being insulted and treated rudely in this process.

Many older workers sneer about millennials, resenting them for taking their opportunities or shoving them aside during the hiring process. If that is you, stop seeing millennials as the enemy. Right now, they are in leadership positions and doing much of the hiring. You must learn to appreciate and work with them or suffer the consequences: an inconsequential career.

Others blame changes within their companies—restructurings, acquisitions, mergers, and outright sales have really shaken up job security.

And while all of those things are to blame, it is time to stop insisting that you have all the skills you need, are delivering more than everybody else, and are being victimized by nasty corporations that favor inexperienced, cheaper employees. Some of that may be true, but honestly, millions of us are so behind in so many areas that others see it as laughable when we claim we are current.

I'm not here to beat you up. I'm here to wake you up so you can succeed again.

This post by "DownTrodden" really summed up what so many people have been experiencing:

"I'm only forty-six, but to employers, I might as well be eighty-six. I only include ten years work experience on my resume. I speak to recruiters and hiring managers on the phone, and they are usually very interested . . . We meet face to face that all goes out the window.

"At my last interview, the CFO was a total jerk. I've only had four full-time jobs in the last twenty years. He kept saying, 'And what did you do before then? And before then? And before then? So when did you graduate college?' I knew I wasn't getting the job. It's been nearly seven weeks now and they keep reposting the position. I've never heard from them. I emailed the recruiter and she said, 'The CFO wants to do some more comparison shopping,' as if I'm a pair of pants at Nordstrom's. Of course, that's code for 'The CFO really wants to find someone exactly like you, but fifteen years younger.' This is a smaller company so I was hoping I would have a chance, but no such luck. The larger companies seem almost pointless to apply to."

Of course that person is "downtrodden." It's hard to stay positive taking that kind of a pounding while trying to get a new job. Companies are often cruel to experienced, accomplished professionals and heartless to those who had the nerve to take a time-out for child-rearing, caregiving, medical reasons, or something else.

It may feel as if the universe is telling you that your career is over, but don't tell yourself that. There is a way. There is a way. There is always a way.

It's not that easy.

But there is a way.

I'll tell you something I hate. It is the statistic for our peak earning age. It's forty-nine for men and forty for women. That's when our salaries stop going up. Salaries generally decrease after forty-five, either by the individual being pushed out or aside, or not being compensated for cost-of-living increases.

Huh?

Did you get that memo? I sure didn't. Most of us just figured our paychecks would keep increasing with our growing experience—all the way to retirement.

And yet here we are.

Fixating on this injustice is useless—and depressing. It's not going to get you hired or promoted; it's just going to frustrate and piss you off. And it will give you an excuse to give up.

Don't give up.

Many, many people are struggling to wage their comebacks. You can pull this off. There is hope, but you have to do some real learning first.

There is no holding your breath or keeping your head low hoping to make it two or five or eight years to the finish line, when you will pack it up and retire. Those who are hunkering down and holding their breath are often the most dispensable people at work. It is time you are born again as a powerful professional with insatiable curiosity who is up on the latest trends and figuring out how to innovate and lead your company into the future.

Those of us who are ready for anything are the ones who will win because we know reality now means never-ending change and we have made up our minds to run faster.

I've always told people how important it is to have a plan because, "That's the greatest piece of fiction you will ever write." Reality has a way of shaking everything up. It can be maddening, and it can fill you with anxiety. But our greatest successes are often born out of what appeared to be our greatest failures.

You have to make a choice: either sit here feeling sorry for yourself, or buck up.

You don't have to look far to find injustice or unfairness at this point in your career. If you haven't experienced it, your friends have.

This book will guide you back into the realm of relevance.

There is more success in your future. You'll have prosperity. You've just got to make up your mind.

This time it is not enough to think positive. You must take action.

Once you make up your mind to do that, you are coming back.

1

Hey, What the Hell Happened to My Career?

This could be you. It could, because if it happened to Trish Johnson, it could happen to any of us.

She's a community leader and a professional who killed it in sales until a bully boss told her, "I can find people a lot younger who can do this for a lot less money."

There was a layoff, a hire, a standoff, a move, more than a thousand online applications and then—nothing. For the longest time. She could not make it past the invisible algorithms of online hiring, and, making it worse, her husband left her for somebody else.

Her unemployment ran out a week before our interview. So much time had lapsed and at age fifty-eight, she found herself on food stamps because the divorce and the back-and-forth with employment had depleted her savings. "Even though I paid for these food stamps with my taxes, it is not easy to take them, and it is not enough to survive on. But it relieves some of the worry." If not for the Affordable Care Act, she would have had no health insurance.

Despite all of those applications in a six-month span, she was invited for just four interviews. She was asked if she'd be able to work for someone younger ("Would they ask a younger person if they could work for someone older?"). She was asked if she was comfortable using technology ("Would they ask that of a younger person?"). They wanted to know what year she graduated high school ("They don't dare ask my age"). They asked her previous salary ("It's way more than a young person would expect").

"You start to lose a little bit of yourself every time somebody rejects you," she said. "You wonder, what am I doing wrong?"

"What am I doing wrong?" That is the refrain I hear over and over and over again from people over age forty whose careers have sputtered out and from people who left the workforce to either stay home with the kids, care for a loved one, explore the world, or find themselves.

How can the business world be so cold, dismissive, and mean to so many good, hardworking, capable human beings who have so much to give?

Every day, new workers enter the workforce who are tech loving, change-embracing, and natural innovators, and they have applied for your job or the job you want.

Yes, they are younger.

But they are also cheaper, don't have as much baggage, and can, in the eyes of many hiring managers, do so much more for so much less.

And they are relevant, which is the real issue.

Age

Our problem isn't that older workers are seen as old. It is that older workers are seen as irrelevant. Unimportant. Of little use. Sadly, "seasoned professional" has come to mean anyone over forty. That's where it all starts. And by the time fifty rolls around? Egad. You assume experience matters, is respected, and is valued. But experience often just means old and out of date.

The New York Times reported on a study that more than half of workers over fifty lose longtime jobs before they are ready to retire. The research, from ProPublica and the Urban Institute, said nine of ten will never achieve their old salary again.

The AARP released an exhaustive study on age discrimination in 2018, reporting that two of three workers over forty-five have seen or experienced age discrimination on the job. Sixty-one percent reported age bias and 91 percent said age discrimination is common.

More than 16 percent of the nearly four thousand people in the study blamed age discrimination when they didn't get a promotion. Seven percent said they were fired, laid off, or forced out because of it.

Age discrimination is rampant. There's no arguing that, so why bother getting stuck in that loop if it is a reality? The more important question is this: what are we going to do about it?

Do statistics condemn you to being a has-been while you still have more that you want to contribute? Do statistics mean you have no chance to earn a decent living until you are ready to retire? Do statistics mean you have to sacrifice your children for your career or your career for your children?

NO. These statistics mean there is a huge problem that impacts many but does *not* defeat all.

It is a brutal reality, but before you start blaming everybody else, you have to own up to your part in it.

There is a perception that older workers are not capable of contributing what younger people contribute, and that people who take time-outs to raise families, give care, or see the world are not as committed as those who don't. There is an expectation that older professionals' salaries are three times as high as younger hires—with no significant return for the extra investment. There is an assumption that they are behind on tech and social media. There are a lot of assumptions, perceptions, and expectations.

Some are unfair stereotypes.

But many of those assumptions are true.

Not everybody is behind, but many people are. It's not enough to be "up" on some things. That's what gets you lumped together with those who aren't up on anything.

If anyone is going to thrive in spite of it, it will be the person who says . . .

"Fuck

This.

I'm

Not

Done."

That's what it comes down to. It's going to be harder than it should be. The whole experience can feel cruel and unfair. But if you make the decision to stop saying, "I'm tech savvy" and actually become tech adventurous, if you stop telling others what you learned and accomplished through experience and instead start reading everything you can on coming trends and how to apply them to your expertise, you are on your way.

Stop bellyaching. Make yourself relevant.

Feel your fury and make up your mind to get back in the ring one more time. There is a way for you to still deliver a knockout punch, but not without a fierce offensive that requires ignoring the inevitable and cruel age bias, confronting the shortcomings you haven't acknowledged, talking to hundreds of strangers, and deciding you are going to win—no matter what.

It's Not Just Age

The issues faced in coming back are similar to what others face when trying to rebuild careers after sabbaticals, gaps for adventure, breaks for caregiving, and time-outs for being stay-at-home parents.

Many employers cheer the daring young people who take a time-out to teach English in Paris or get another degree or hike the Pacific Crest Trail. Especially when those career gaps can be framed to show growth and learning that will be helpful in leadership, hiring managers are intrigued and willing to at least consider the person for the job.

But a three- or five-year or even longer intermission is another story, and the fallout from such a gap is the same faced by many stay-at-home parents when they try to come back.

This headline in the *Harvard Business Review* is quite jarring: "Stay-at-Home Moms are Half as Likely to Get a Job Interview as Moms Who Got Laid Off." The article is written and based on research by sociology professor Kate Weisshaar at the University of North Carolina, Chapel Hill.

Weisshaar sent 3,374 made-up résumés that looked like they were coming from employed people with no work-history gaps, unemployed people, and stay-at-home parents. Names represented both genders. The résumés described applicants equally experienced with skills and job history. Those with gaps in employment had been out for eighteen months. Weisshaar used these fake résumés to apply for jobs as accountants, financial analysts, software engineers, HR managers, and marketing directors in fifty U.S. cities. She tracked who got interview requests and who didn't.

What happened?

A little over 15 percent of employed moms, nearly 10 percent of unemployed moms, and only 5 percent of stay-at-home moms got callbacks. Same thing for fathers.

Why? Weisshaar concluded that stay-at-home applicants were perceived as less capable. There was an assumption that their skills were rusty. But the bias went deeper. She reported, "Respondents viewed stay-at-home parents as less reliable, less deserving of a job, and—the biggest penalty—less committed to work, compared with unemployed applicants. Interestingly . . . stay-at-home fathers are perceived as even less committed and reliable than stay-at-home mothers. This could be because fathers face expectations to provide for their families and respondents viewed stay-at-home fathers negatively for not adhering to these expectations."

Well, that sucks.

But again, are you going to surrender to that perception or figure out what it takes to be in the 5 percent getting the callbacks?

#hasbeen

I recently saw some text messages between a midlevel manager and his boss's boss. The manager was kissing up and trying to undermine his direct boss. He referred to his boss as "#hasbeen." It was biting and cruel, but also emblematic of the dismissive attitudes of those who judge us in the workplace.

You've got it, or you don't. You're in, or you're out.

You will hear one word from me over and over again. It is RELEVANCE. If you aren't consistently seeking it, you are #hasbeen. And that is not where you need to be if you hope to maintain a successful career or stage a triumphant comeback.

Are You a #hasit or #hasbeen?

Ask yourself:

- Have you stopped to honestly, critically examine whether your skills are as current and useful as the younger people around you?
- Have you taken charge of your own education and

development? What classes have you completed in the last year—on your own—to deepen your grasp on change in your industry?

- Do you know what's coming on the horizon? Have you studied the latest trends that will come over the next two, five, and ten years? Do you talk about that at work, making it clear you are contributing to that future?
- Have you come up with a strategy to put yourself in front of it?
- Are you reading the right newsletters, engaging in online discussions, getting daily Google alerts for the right keywords that update you constantly?
- Are you constantly engaging with younger people, helping them but letting *them* mentor *you*?
- Have you had a makeover? You have to look like a player. Stop dressing by default.
- Have you updated your personal brand every year and strategically communicated what you are contributing that no one else can offer?
- Are you reading what your CEO and top leaders are reading?
- Have you volunteered for committees or assignments that give you exposure and new leadership opportunities?
- Are you consistently updating your boss on what you are working on?
- Are you expanding your network and calling in chits?

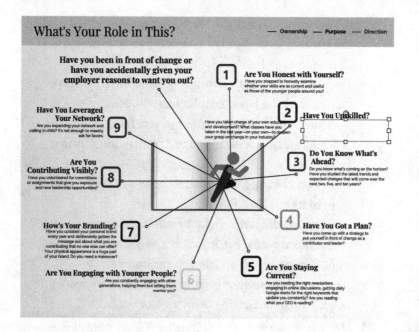

How Did This Slide Happen?

If you can't handle the tough-love truth about your own role in what has happened to your career, don't expect to climb back on top.

As a generation, baby boomers dabbled in tech but didn't keep pace with the kids who were playing Nintendo in the womb. Tech was impersonal and, at times, frustrating or annoying. The Internet was cool. Email was convenient. But change kept coming. It was hard enough to keep up with Facebook, without worrying about Twitter and Instagram and LinkedIn and Snapchat, TikTok, YouTube, Reddit, Pinterest, and dozens of other social media platforms. Boomers went from being amazed that they could have a computer in their homes to having a computer thousands of times faster and more powerful that fit in their hands, made phone calls, took pictures, and connected them 24/7 with everybody, everywhere.

They slowly danced with change, not noticing that the day came when they didn't know enough about how to use that tech to innovate and drive change. Millennials showed up in the workplace and didn't play by the rules. Boomers (and some Gen Xers) groused about the work habits or tone or dress of this new generation, but the millennials kept showing up and delivering.

Time passed. Boomers lagged. Millennials kept delivering and didn't care if others didn't like their work style.

What happened to the rules? The decorum? Younger people thought nothing of bounding into the CEO's office to share an idea or complain about something. That seemed rude to the rule players, but it is acceptable and even encouraged in many workplaces now. It wouldn't have been tolerated if those young people weren't delivering, but they were delivering.

Then this happened: the honchos realized that younger people who were being paid substantially less than loyal, veteran employees were contributing substantially more.

Who were they going to bet on?

Business is business. It's not about loyalty; it's about money. Some companies have hearts, but many don't.

As millennials aged, they started taking leadership opportunities that boomers thought were theirs by right. Now, millennials are the bosses.

OK boomer.

How frustrating it is for those older people who still resent millennials to now have to report to them. That kind of tension is not going to create opportunity and success.

Boomers and Gen Xers grew up with clear career expectations: get out of school, get a job, work hard, move up. Respect others, play nicely, honor the hierarchy, and then your turn will come.

But, in the end, instead of being rewarded, the older employees were shoved aside and mocked behind their backs.

Or fired.

And not hired elsewhere.

Coming Back

The time has come to buck up, regroup, and start being a victor instead of a victim. What can you do to insulate your career? If you are trying to find work, how can you be sure that you are the first hired and last fired? How can you raise your profile so you are a known value?

Companies discriminate. People discriminate.

It is an ego-crushing experience made a little less painful when you realize it is not personal. Yes, it's unfair, and it's terribly wrong. But do you want to spend your time bellyaching, or are you ready to recalibrate so you can experience huge opportunities? If you think age or an employment gap is the issue, you are still the same, strong, and brilliant person you once were, but you have fallen into the same trap that has baited most of the people in your situation. It is time to look in the mirror and do a tough self-examination to see whether you truly are relevant compared to a new, less expensive hire. If your life choice to take a time-out has made coming back hard, you have to figure out how the game has changed in order to play it.

We no longer have the luxury of turning up our noses at the changes trending in modern culture. We can't ignore technological challenges—even when they are utterly confusing. We can't complain about millennials.

Many years ago, I'd get so annoyed when my younger friends would not answer the phone when I knew it was right there in their hands. They'd text instead of call. It ticked me off. I finally asked one of them, "Why do you do that?" And she said,

"Because it saves time. Nobody wants to talk on the phone anymore." She was right. I finally evolved. I wasn't the first or the last to make the change. I now know that when change is coming, those who adapt first are the survivors. Instead of judging change, we need to check it out instead of stubbornly holding to old ways.

Many of us used to take a pass on social media because it wasn't as personal as picking up the phone and actually talking to somebody. But time moved on without us, and most finally relented and got on board. Remember when people kept saying, "I don't need to post something every time I use the bathroom"? Well, it was never about posting your toilet habits or pictures of what you ate for dinner, and those who avoided social media fell drastically behind. Resistance wasn't the matter of pride many thought it was. Those who thought they were waiting out a trend were wrong. Resistance was very, very costly to personal and professional relevance. They were branding themselves as #hasbeen.

It is a tough moment for older workers, but remember this: some older people are winning at this. Is that by accident or intention? They are ageless, ass-kicking, unrelenting contributors who will not be stopped. They forced themselves to be heard, so they got on the radar as relevant, viable, and valuable—just what companies want in the workplace of the future.

They had the one thing that leader after leader told me was mandatory for long-term career survival: insatiable curiosity.

You're going to need it.

You have much to learn, but you can learn it.

Don't freak out.

First, start looking at artificial intelligence, machine learning, blockchain, robotics, and big data. Study them to figure out how they will impact your job and workplace.

The process can seem intimidating and confusing, but here is the good news: there are plenty of tools to help. There are YouTube videos and courses on everything. You need to learn LinkedIn? There are videos! There are free courses from the best universities in the world that will tell you everything you need to learn.

I wanted to get some basic understanding on where we are with artificial intelligence (AI), robotics, and blockchain. It literally took a few hours. Blockchain was confusing to me, and I watched three videos that totally confused me. Then I looked at one titled, "How to explain blockchain to a child." I got it!

Once you understand the basics, you can go deeper. You have to admit that you are behind if you are ever going to catch up. Know what's going on out there and use it to your advantage because, sadly, it will lead to your peril if you don't.

If you don't take ownership over some of your obstacles, then you can't find your way past them. As hard as it is to admit this, much of what is hindering our careers is our own fault.

Don't flog yourself for falling behind, for not reacting quickly enough, for holding on to what was, for being treated poorly at work. We are the first to face this velocity of change. Let go of what you did or didn't do. Just realize that not rising up was costly to you, and make up your mind that you are taking charge again. Whether the challenge is old skills or what may have changed while you were out of the office on leave, it's time to dive in and swim fast.

This is your call to action. It is going to take work. But if you follow through and take the steps required to redefine your relevance, you will find your career moving forward again. It'll be a different career because everyone's career is different.

The truth I share in this book comes from frank interviews with hundreds of our nation's most influential CEOs, senior executives, business leaders, seasoned professionals, academics, organizational experts, and psychologists.

A radio interviewer asked me, "Who will be the biggest critic of your theories?"

"Anyone who would rather be a victim," I answered.

If you choose to blame others for your struggles, you're not going to embrace a solution that demands up-front accountability. You don't have to beat yourself up because you aren't where you should be regarding technology, trends, and innovation. MILLIONS of your peers are just as far behind. But the time has come to accept what is, then act.

It's a hell of a lot easier to blame discrimination than it is to blame yourself. You probably aren't as up on things as you think, and if you do everything possible to update yourself, you have much more to offer.

Is this harder than what our parents faced? You bet. The rules were clear and they knew what they had to do. A job could last an entire career; now they never do. But you can continue to contribute at the highest level, to matter, to keep your job, to have a thriving career and make a difference. What you must do is seek what is uncomfortable, unclear, and uncertain.

Proving Yourself. Again. Argh.

We have to make up our minds to be part of the revolution and evolution of work, rather than reacting to it. The reactors get left behind, especially when they are older.

If you keep doing what you've always done, hoping it will work, well, good luck with that.

It won't work.

"If you are assuming you are going to hide underneath the radar so the force of change won't hit you, it will hit you really hard when it does hit you," said Tom Greco, president and CEO of Advance Auto Parts. "I don't care how old anybody is. Some of those who think they are discriminated against may actually be getting replaced because they aren't hungry anymore. I see a thirty-one-year-old that I want to kick in the rear end, and I see a vice president at sixty-five who has a lot of energy. There's no coasting anymore. Those jobs don't exist."

Get in front of the change, he said.

"You have to look at all of this transformation as a positive thing," said Greco, who is also the former CEO of FritoLay. "How do you influence it and become a part of it? How do you think about it? What kinds of skills do you need? I want to be out front, understanding what is happening. I want to be a part of the change instead of responding to the change."

The transformation is occurring, he said. It won't happen overnight, "But this is going to be as big as the industrial revolution in terms of what work gets done. In the next three to five years, there will be a very different way we work."

Are you still delivering like you are hungry to perform?

Facebook is being sued for age discrimination by a sixty-one-year-old Manhattan man. He says top executives stopped aggressively recruiting him after they got his résumé and saw that he graduated from Dartmouth in 1978. He was told the position had suddenly closed.

His lawsuit uses a widely quoted speech by CEO Mark Zuckerberg, who, it is reported, told an audience at Stanford: "Young people are just smarter." The suit claims that shows a climate perfectly ripe for age discrimination.

I'm actually glad if Zuckerberg said that. It shows what we are up against. He illuminated what is widely assumed in the corporate world today.

Young = smart. Old = done.

#hasbeen

If you are still working, do not get complacent! You may be killing it on the job today and getting spectacular results, but companies aren't as focused on today as they were. They are obsessed with tomorrow. They try to determine what you will contribute in five or ten years when technology has changed everything again.

It doesn't matter if you are the best person for the job today. You might be. But that is not enough.

We have to change our mindset and the perception others have of us, then dive into the opportunities that will exist once we come up with our new strategy.

It's not failure when you realize that your career has stopped working or you find yourself struggling to get hired. You have not failed. Maybe you failed to keep up, but my bet is that you worked very hard, did your best, and produced great results. You can't help wondering why all of your hard work added up to a kick in the gut. But you either confront what must be done or continue to be minimized.

Then There's Race

If you google "age discrimination and race," you won't find much of anything. It's hard to sort out which factor is the obstacle, but perhaps minority professionals don't fixate on the age issue as much because they have had to overcome biases and discrimination throughout their careers.

"It is sometimes difficult for white men and women who get to be middle-aged and all of a sudden hit the wall. They're like, 'What happened?' But if you are a person of color, you have been experiencing challenges every day of your life," said Trudy Bourgeois, CEO of the Center for Workforce Excellence. Her books, speaking, and consulting made her a national expert on leadership development, diversity and inclusion, and workplace transformation. "It is just another bump in the road for you. It doesn't hit you as hard emotionally because it's not your first time being marginalized, being denied equal access or equal opportunity. This is your life. So you draw on all of these experiences that you've had to give yourself the right mindset and say, 'I've just got to find the right opportunity.' But if you have never experienced it, you don't have anything to draw on."

What does she do when she hits the wall?

"First, I pray," Bourgeois said, "and then I look at myself. I can't change anybody else. I can only change myself. I go inward."

She shares an internal dialogue that will be helpful to so many others because you have to take ownership before you can fix the problem. "Ask yourself, 'What led you here? Were you not paying attention? Were you not on top of your game? Were you not studying the market? Were you not even listening? When I do hit the wall, it's usually because I've been so busy working I'm not paying attention. You have to look deep within and then say, 'Okay, what are you going to do? What do you want to do?'"

For minorities, the layers of discrimination become increasingly complex with age, said China Widener, a principal at Deloitte who is a leader in diversity and inclusion. Minority professionals have always had extra obstacles on the track from the beginning of the race. Once they hit middle age, there are a few more. It's best to just find a way past the obstacles.

"You get to a point where you have to do battle with what I'll call *public perceptions* of what age really means: whether you are still quick, whether you are up to speed, whether you are technologically advanced, whether you are keeping up with the flow of information in your chosen particular field. If there is already a question because you are a woman or a minority as to whether or not you bring, if you will, the goods, that gets exacerbated when age is on top of it. There are things we should do, and ought to do to remain relevant and aware, but you cannot underestimate the cumulative effect of those layers. The gender question matters. The race question matters."

The Financial Hit

Sadly, much of this has financial implications because, when you get derailed, your paycheck is impacted. Sometimes people are demoted or lose their jobs and spend months or even years trying to find something comparable. Often it takes more than one transition to get close to the paycheck you once had, and there are millions of stories of people who never rebound to that place. I interviewed a woman who lost a job that paid her a very healthy six-figure salary. After months without income, she started working in a dress shop.

These are crucible moments when you are forced to define your resilience.

Nobody who plans on retiring in their sixties expects to be tossed out five or ten years early and to experience a devastating pay cut that diminishes their savings and affects the level of comfort they can anticipate in retirement.

Young moms who take a few years to stay home, planning to come back, don't expect it to take so long to get hired and return to where they once were. Or to be so judged in the process.

When you confront a financial emergency like this, you feel a degree of desperation. You may fear money is going to run out, and you have to do something RIGHT NOW.

So few resolutions come quickly or easily. Often, you've got to take a short-term detour to stop the financial hemorrhage. But don't accept a short-term fix as a real fix. It's not. Don't give in and don't give up.

This is a long-term proposition.

It'll work, but you've got to work it.

Rise up.

We have to do some very strategic guerilla networking.

And we must have something to pitch, which means we have to catch up to the future—and quickly. That begins with a few months of concentrated immersion into your industry trends, technology, innovation, and communication strategies. After you catch up, everything gets so much easier. This doesn't mean mastering the technology you are using today. That's a given. Success requires figuring out what is coming so you are first to be ready for what is coming in the next two, five, and ten years. Once you are caught up, it won't be nearly as hard to maintain your future relevance.

Either confront what must be done or continue to be minimized and, perhaps, cast out.

You've succeeded in the past—you'll succeed again. Period.

I touched base with Trish Johnson today, and she's happy, employed, and off food stamps. After more than a thousand applications, she landed in huge success.

This story is hopeful and inspiring. She is now soaring in a sales job making more money than she has ever made. She paid off her debts and bought a car with cash. She's even socked away some money for retirement.

Trish is the oldest person on the company payroll, and found her way in with the help of someone she knew. She pushed her network until it delivered. Networking is nothing new, but the hard push is new to many of us.

"He knew my worth," she said, "which shows you again: It's who you know."

2

The Death of Experience

Renee Lay had exceeded her sales goals by millions, scored above expectations on all of her annual reviews, and suddenly someone with far less experience became her boss. That was supposed to be *her* job. Soon, she missed another promotion that went to somebody with little experience.

Lay, who'd been at her company in senior roles for more than a decade, demanded an explanation and scheduled a meeting.

The meeting was canceled. So was the next. She kept pushing to get together with her boss to talk about her career. Finally able to confront him, she wanted to know what was holding her back.

He hemmed, he hawed, and then blurted: "You have so much old trash in your head. We wanted someone without that in their heads so we could look at different routes for the business to grow."

"Trash? This is not trash. This is years of on-the-job experience," she answered. "If you consider it trash, I just don't understand that."

She hung in there with that major corporation (which you likely know and love) for a miserably long time because she didn't want to be middle-aged and competing with all the other middle-aged people who were struggling to get new jobs.

"I feel like I have been put out to pasture," she told me at the time. Every day, she did her job. She exceeded every goal that was set for her. The new hires weren't keeping pace with her. "I am keeping my head down, keeping a smile on my face, and just continuing to do what I do," she told me.

Several months later, she underwent major surgery. Ten days after she returned to work, her "position was eliminated."

Wheeler was the sole breadwinner in the house. She still had a son in high school. She *had* to find work, which she did, at a much smaller company. To get that job, she took a $50,000 pay cut. She knows how lucky she was to even find that position, but she is still angry at the company she had so loyally served.

Why would one of the largest corporations in the world turn its back on experience?

Because that company is no different from most other companies these days.

What we are witnessing is the death of experience.

Do not . . .

And, I mean this . . .

Do. *NOT.* Say:

"But I have so much experience . . ."

"I have decades of experience . . ."

"You can't learn what I know just coming out of school . . ."

"We do this and it works. If it ain't broke, don't fix it."

You worked your whole life to be as smart and able as you are right now, but using your experience to justify your value is a huge mistake in a professional culture that often equates the word "experience" with the words "has-been." The consultants are helping companies design the "workplace of the future," and apparently the words "experience" and "future" don't mesh.

Experience used to be what counted most, but employers

now expect that you have experience. They can't stand it when you prattle on about it as proof of your worth.

Telling people how many years of experience you have doesn't advertise that you are better, it just advertises that you are older.

They don't care about your experience. They care about your abilities and how you are growing your abilities to drive the company into the future.

I'm being blunt and direct here. Not all CEOs think this way, but many, many of them do. Not all companies function like this, but many, many of them do. And that is why so many veteran employees are sinking.

Why Experience Doesn't Drive Success Anymore

Oxford University professors studied technology and workplace trends and concluded that 47 percent of today's jobs will vanish in the next ten to twenty years because so much of what we are doing now will be automated and replaced by computers, artificial intelligence, or robots.

Stop. Did that sink in?

FORTY-SEVEN PERCENT OF TODAY'S JOBS WILL BE GONE.

The reason that study and its follow-up were so painful to read is that researchers warned professionals to stop operating in a middle layer of awareness, knowing things have changed dramatically, pretending they are aware of it all, but not realizing *everything* has changed. *Everything.* So many people are recklessly counting on outdated or useless skills to define their worth at work.

The skills that used to last an average of thirty-two years after college now barely last at all, with the "half-life" of job skills degrading to as little as two years now, depending on the industry or specialty.

So the fact that you have experience in things people no longer care about or do makes employers shrug and say, "So what?"

Zach Friedman, an innovator for Nationwide, nails it: "What worked before might not work today," he said. "If you have thirty years of irrelevant experience and a millennial has two years of relevant experience, he or she is the expert."

Well, there you have it. And then there's the fact that technology is making all of us less relevant every day.

Deloitte issued a recent report that said 67 percent of CEOs believe technology will create more value than human capital. Forty-four percent of large global corporations say robotics, automation, and AI "will make people 'largely irrelevant' in the future of work."

If you want to depress yourself even more, read that last sentence twice.

The change is here, but many workers still don't realize it. It is important to take advantage of the humanlike opportunities in the workplace, but I expect that to change as AI gets more human. My phone tells me jokes. Alexa on my Amazon Echo tells me to have a nice day, pays me compliments, asks me trivia, and even farted when one of my friends told her to.

I have a troubling relationship with Alexa. I use "her" to set deadlines and timers as I work and catch myself actually thanking "her" out loud when "she" gives me an alert or turns on a light. As if she were a person.

Change is here. Robots and AI are too human. As professionals, that makes us vulnerable.

It's going to impact your career.

Be Insatiably Curious

If you aren't changing with the change, you're done.

Canadian prime minister Justin Trudeau crystallized that

fact when he said, "The pace of change has never been this fast, yet it will never be this slow again."

There is no greater example of how quickly things can change than what happened when the workplace literally re-created itself *overnight* when the COVID-19 lockdowns began. In an instant, nearly every working professional started working from home. Meetings went virtual. And, just like that, companies realized they were able to keep things moving without the cost or hassle of traditional office space. The process of going virtual likely skipped five or ten years of easing into that change. Everyone was forced to accept, cope, and adapt.

All of us have had to deal with rapid change because it has been such a constant for so long. Those who adapt fastest are rewarded with greater opportunities.

"That's just the world all of us are living in," said Carolyn Tastad, Procter & Gamble group president for North America. "You have to have a curiosity. In a world that operates so quickly, it becomes more and more important. You have to be curious. You have to continue to learn to do things differently. You have to be technology savvy. Be self-sufficient. All of those things help you keep up with the world and the pace at which it goes today."

The Deloitte workforce study found that millennials rank training and development as the most important benefit of their jobs—nearly four times as important as greater vacation time. That shows that young people value and are always seeking to expand their skill sets. Keeping current matters to them.

Many leaders no longer view thirty years of experience as a plus. It's seen as thirty years of "repetitive experience" that has become too expensive because of annual salary increases that culminated in an employee that delivers less value than someone with little experience but more technological acuity.

Shouldn't decades of loyal service to a company count for something?

Of course they should, if this were all about being fair or nice, but it isn't. That loyal service often doesn't mean much—especially in a climate where many corporations *want* you to keep moving along.

In fact, job longevity can actually be seen as a detriment. When you've been playing in one sandbox for a very, very long time, it may be that your vision is too limited to that one perspective. You have to demonstrate that you have imaginative, useful perspective, and that is usually the by-product of working in a variety of companies with a variety of people.

"I always look at my résumé and ask what have I done that I learned *this year,*" said Kimberly Ross, the former chief financial officer of Avon, Ahold, and Baker Hughes who currently serves on several major national corporate boards. It is all about your expertise. Old expertise is not worth much, and Ross knows it and takes action herself. "If I can't add a new discipline or experience that I gained this year, then I kick myself and say, 'What do I need to go get involved with?' If you can't add some meaningful experience and learning every year, it is an indication that something needs to be done."

The way experience becomes a plus is when you can show that you have delivered more every single year by driving trends, not reacting to them.

If you've been too passive in that department, it is time to play catch-up. You must get up to speed, period. The good news is that the very technology that has put you behind is a fabulous tool for catching you up and moving you forward.

There are certain jobs where employers demand experience. You don't want to get in a jumbo jet with a pilot who hasn't flown before. You don't want a surgeon who has never done surgery.

But there are many times when people rise to positions of power when they don't have the experience that was once expected.

Find ways to boost your expertise with current advancements and show that your experience gives you the confidence and insight to use that new technology better than anyone else. If not, find ways to demonstrate that you are the best to manage and lead the people who are using the technology.

"If you don't translate your experience into contributing something of relevance, your experience doesn't matter," said Jill Smart, president of the National Academy of Human Resources and the former chief human resources officer for Accenture, which has more than 450,000 employees.

"You have to be able to contribute something people want you to contribute. If they don't think it is relevant, it's not worth anything," she said.

You can boast of always meeting or exceeding your numbers, "But meeting number goals may not be the most relevant thing. If you don't have potential for the future, then I really should put somebody in your job so they get the experience you are getting because they are going to be there contributing in the future. If I don't see you growing into the future, then I am wasting that spot. What is more important? Somebody delivering today that I don't believe will deliver tomorrow? Or somebody who doesn't have the track record of success today who I can prepare for the future?"

I know, I know. Younger people leave jobs before that future ever arrives. But companies are still obsessed with their people's place on the runway to the future.

Whether you are pushing your career forward at your current job or trying to find a job elsewhere, stop hollering, "But I have so much experience!" and start presenting a case for applying your abilities to the challenges of tomorrow.

"If you are relying only on what you did in the past instead of growing, creating, innovating, and coming up with new ideas, then you are not the person I want in that spot," Smart said. "When someone says, 'It's the way we've always done it and it's been working,' well, that's a bad answer. It may have worked in the past and it might work right now, but will it work in the future? Or is there also something better?"

Why Experience "Ain't What It Used to Be"

Someone who has voracious curiosity and is always learning and trying (and sometimes failing) at new and wild things is much more attractive to a company than somebody with a lengthy track record of showing up and performing for decades, tried and true.

People don't enjoy hearing you ramble on about some similar situation you dealt with years ago because most of those stories aren't relevant. They want your knowledge, not your stories, and your knowledge must be 100 percent current. They want to hear your ideas for solutions based on what is happening today and future trends and challenges. If you don't know the lingo of today and tomorrow, you are not a player. You can get caught up!

Remember this: success is based on your ability, not your track record.

"There's less and less time for people who dig in and say, 'It's always worked this way,'" said Shelley Broader, former CEO of Chicos FAS and former CEO of Walmart in its EMEA region, which included Europe, the Middle East, sub-Saharan Africa, and Canada. "It's important to know how it usually works and how it worked in the past, but that doesn't mean it's going to work that way in the future. It's like freezing yourself in an era."

The way to demonstrate your expertise is to constantly gain more. Read the right books, magazines, and news stories. Sprinkle hints of your awareness of future trends into conversation easily and frequently. Show that you are growing your expertise and ability every day. Once you are viewed as forward-thinking, your experience actually does come into play as a delineating factor. Your past experience then may give you a relevant perspective *and* an edge.

But if you can't strut your immediate and future relevance, you are demonstrating your irrelevance. Falling back on how much experience you have can suggest that you cling to old achievements and old times to define your worth. Again, the corporate world doesn't care about what happened in the olden days (and sadly, that can mean more than five years ago) because it is unlikely to happen again.

Few companies put a premium on "institutional memory" because that's just a memory of what was and it's institutional.

Two arenas that do require experience are leadership and communication, especially when helping younger people who count on technology to connect with others. Seasoned professionals know the human element. But they face increasing difficulty operating in that arena because they have not gained the expertise that shows their people that they know what it will take to move forward and drive or play on a cutting-edge team. Basically, get current and go future; then people will listen to you.

Yes, it is insulting that your years of experience don't get the respect you think they deserve. It is not fair, but it is neither unique to you nor the result of disrespect from a singular, nasty boss. It is just the way things are. Companies want people who know how to steer in a thick fog of the unknown. They care about the bottom line and often don't see nurturing a human connection to that as valuable or their duty. They may know that happy and fulfilled people deliver more, but that fact tends to pale with the reality that younger employees with less experience have the agility and ingenuity to see current situations for the potential they hold for the future.

And younger people likely will reach that potential for less money than someone who has been on the payroll forever.

"We are living in a Darwinian age," said Neela Montgomery, CEO of Crate and Barrel. "Those who are intellectually curious, self-learners have far more important qualities than expertise. Expertise is something, no offense, that a computer can do better these days—myself included. How do you solve problems, think conceptually, and acquire knowledge you don't have? Obviously, experience counts, but it ain't what it used to be."

Experience No Longer Means You Know Better
Back in the day, seniority and years of experience mattered greatly. People started in the mailroom and tried to work up into the corner office. They paid their dues.

That paradigm no longer exists, said Todd Cherches, an expert on management and leadership who teaches at both New York University and Columbia University while consulting on generational and management issues. "Nobody wants or is getting a gold watch for many years of service," he said. "If you are a twenty-seven-year-old HR person and you see the résumé of someone who is fifty-eight, well, that's your parents' age. It used to be that the recruiter was the parents' age."

Cherches adds, "A millennial doesn't have twenty-five years of experience, but is that long experience even valued anymore? When a boomer says, 'When I was at IBM in 1978 . . .' millennials are already falling asleep. In the old days, that meant something. Now that works against you. I have a friend who was passed over for a number of promotions who was told, 'You've been here too long.' You are looked at as a dinosaur instead of someone who has built up intellectual capital over that twenty-five years. It works against you."

So you may be unknowingly killing your future by clinging

to old experience that supports the status quo rather than the constant of change.

William Arruda, an expert and author on personal branding, warns not to make your experience the totality of your brand.

"Experience is great, it's an asset, but unfortunately it is not enough to tip the scale for you over others," he said. "Experience is one piece of it. You can click that box a hundred times. It's a little differentiating, but it is not differentiating enough to get people excited about you. So you have to say, what can I bring in addition to that experience? You probably have confidence. Confidence is a great thing. Are you willing to take risks? What are the other things that will make you super compelling?"

If you are counting on experience to prove that you know better, you should stop for a moment and ask if that's correct. In many cases, it isn't. Knowing better requires a track record of actively upskilling and chasing relevance. If you count on your company to keep you current on technology and trends, you are making a terrible mistake. You are falling behind the people who are driving innovation and change every day.

Read. Study. Learn. Repeat.

How Have You Upskilled Today?

As you choose how you upskill, look into the future and study what you are going to be able to deliver in five or ten years, because it is probable that the skills you have mastered for today will not be cutting edge tomorrow.

The McKinsey Global Institute studied how artificial intelligence would impact the workplace and concluded that it could replace upward of 30 percent of the human labor in the world. The study estimates that by 2030, between four hundred and eight hundred million jobs will be replaced by technology.

It doesn't matter how good you are or how smart or reliable.

You are not only competing against people. You are competing with robots and computers.

I delude myself when I say, "Well, a computer isn't going to replace me because it won't do interviews and research and put it all together in a book. And nobody wants to hear a robot do a motivational speech," but, at this very minute, computers are scanning data and *writing news articles by themselves.* I just asked Alexa to motivate me. "A journey of a thousand miles begins with a single step," she said. I just read this headline on Variety's website: "Hollywood is Banking that a Robot Named Erica can be the Next Movie Star."

It seems absurd, but it is very, very real.

Much of the legal profession is being reduced to an algorithm, although I can't imagine a computer or robot effectively delivering a closing argument. Artificial intelligence will make junior lawyer jobs hard to find, but a junior lawyer with a computer science degree will be very appealing to those doing the hiring.

Doctors are using this intelligence every day. Robots are doing surgery!

This is a new world. It is expected that most data entry jobs will disappear at a rapid rate. Same with customer service.

It's not looking good for taxi, Lyft, and Uber drivers because self-driving vehicles are all around us now. Flying cars are coming. I can't believe I just wrote that sentence, but I did because it is true. They exist.

It is crazy to think that computers and robots and drones can literally replace the people who cook, serve, and deliver food in restaurants—but that technology exists and is being perfected. I am not sure how I would feel, sitting at a table and getting my burger dropped in front of me by a drone, but it is happening already in Asia.

We are now checking ourselves out at the store. Think of how many jobs that has eliminated.

This is our world. It is a sci-fi reality, and if we want to succeed in it, we have to learn.

Mind-boggling, right?

So you can see why company leaders get annoyed when we are indignant that our past experience doesn't count anymore.

The truth is that many of us built our house of expertise on the strongest possible foundation, but the ground shifted.

Crate and Barrel's Montgomery said what's coming may be hard, but it must be addressed up front so people can be prepared.

"It is irresponsible of us as leaders to put people in a position where they don't understand reality. That is not being a kind leader, that is being a complicit leader. With my team, I have to tell them that setting people up to fail is not ethically right. We have to sometimes confront the fact that some people cannot adapt the skill set or their mindset. We will support them to gain new skills or support them to transition. We have some of those conversations coming."

Several leaders told me there is some discomfort in this transition because it can seem as cold as it does progressive. Your experience may not be valued, but it is still worth something.

Are You Inactive, Active, Proactive, or Superproactive?

Workplace expert Cherches says it's on you to take charge of your future because the technology you know today will be obsolete tomorrow. If you don't know the next big thing, you are lost.

So he asks, Are you inactive, active, proactive, or super-proactive?

"If you are inactive, you don't do anything. You sit and hope it goes away, but it doesn't. Reactive means you are responsive.

When something happens, you respond to it. The problem with that is you quickly fall behind and are always a step behind. It's like Lucille Ball in the chocolate factory," he said, conjuring up the classic scene in *I Love Lucy* where she falls so behind in wrapping chocolates from a conveyer belt, she stuffs them in her clothes and mouth to hide them. "The conveyer belt is going faster and faster and you can't keep up with the pace. If you are active, you are keeping up with the pace. You are ready, it happens, you respond in real time. Proactive means you are a step ahead. You are anticipating and even initiating it. And superproactive is thinking five steps ahead. It is not anticipating tomorrow or next week but next year or three years from now. That is where being a leader comes in. Be a thought leader instead of a thought follower."

If you are standing still, you are falling behind. You need to move. That means constantly reading, taking courses, talking to people, always asking questions. You have to seize the initiative and own it.

"You need to take the initiative and be responsible for your own future," he said. "That means reading, watching videos, spotting trends. It's almost overwhelming how much is out there, but decide what is the next level for you. What are you interested in? What do you want to be known as the guru of, or the go-to person for?

"It *is* overwhelming," he said. "You can only do the tip of the iceberg, but what is that for you? What are you going to focus on to make yourself relevant and valuable? If you are the best in the world at something that doesn't matter anymore, where does that leave you? You have to be at the forefront of technology, leverage social media, and keep networking."

You do have one advantage in your experience arsenal.

It's you. You are human.

Somebody has to deal with the people who are dealing with all of the automation. Your people skills are especially valuable in a technologically driven workplace, said Ken Burdick, CEO of WellCare, which provides health-care coverage for nearly 4.5 million people.

"The 'I've been there and done that' experience is becoming less and less useful," he said. "It's not going to be how fast you can build a spreadsheet that will determine your professional success. It will be much more important to have the softer skills. With artificial intelligence and big data, all transactional things are going to be automated. The ability to communicate is going to become so much more important because so much of the routine will be the world of bots and artificial intelligence. So the most important dimension of business is going to be for those areas where it takes difficult conversation, compromise, seeking out diverse perspectives and experiences, listening well, and bringing the best out of people. Those are the skills that we will never be able to automate, and those are ultimately the keys to running a successful business."

The more people work remotely, he said, the more those skills come into play because "it raises the premium on being an effective communicator and inspiring people to work."

Those are the skills that many more veteran employees possess because they always had to communicate with people directly. So if you are seeking a leadership role, play up those timeless human skills. But realize you will not be tapped for leadership assignments if you can't comprehend the technology and change your people are dealing with.

"What separates one company from the other is the way you can bring people together with passion and energy and commitment and dedication pursuing the same objective," Burdick said.

Synchrony CEO Margaret M. Keane says she has to figure out how to use AI to proactively train and upskill employees if she is going to adapt to the future of work.

"We are moving very fast in the transformation of the workforce," she said. "We're going to be giving new hires jobs that they aren't 100 percent ready for. That demographic shift is occurring and those young people have to be comfortable enough to ask for help and advice."

Sometimes, if you cling too tightly to your experience, your only relevance exists in your ability to train your replacement. Sad, but true. It is far better that you scan what is happening and going to happen, then figure out your role as a change leader.

When I was in college, we studied "teletext," the seed of what would become the Internet. When I interviewed for a reporting job right out of school, I asked the newspaper's executive editor what the paper was planning in terms of teletext projects.

He looked at me like I was crazy and admitted he didn't know what the hell teletext even was. He was a classic journalist, a hard-bitten editor, with tons of experience. He had no clue about the future. That paper and so many others have been all but destroyed by the Internet. The entire industry was in denial.

Regardless of your industry, there's no sitting anything out and no point hanging on to the old rules.

If you cling to "right now" professionally, you miss all the possibility and magic of what is coming, and that is where you will find opportunity and success.

Other people are frozen, not knowing what to do.

Just go learn something new. Then learn something else. One step at a time, you'll become relevant.

3

Evolve

Marissa Mayer got hung up on the Motorola Startac, her first cell phone. Mayer started her career as one of Google's earliest and most impactful leaders and then went on to become the CEO of Yahoo! and cofounder of Lumi Labs, a company that is finding consumer applications for artificial intelligence.

But, way back when, Mayer bought that Startac and loved the satisfying click it made when she closed it. It was the phone of choice for every TV show character, and the thing was indestructible—almost. After two years, her phone screen developed an LCD bleed—a big, black smear, and all she could read were the first few letters of people's names. She lived with that for a while, but when she went to get a new phone, she learned Motorola had stopped manufacturing it.

"You could get a new one on eBay and keep using this phone that you really love," someone in the Sprint store told her.

"So I did that. I bought a new Motorola Startac and, about a year later, when that one broke, I bought another one on eBay," she told me. "Then I started to worry that I would run out of my back supply of Motorola Startacs, so I started buying more and more of them so I could have a new Motorola Startac every year or two."

She'd found a way to cling to the past and make it work. But then she realized something. Hoarding a bunch of outdated cell phones was absurd.

She was twenty-nine and her goal was to live to be more than a hundred.

"I was stockpiling Motorola Startacs. Did I really think I could buy a lifetime supply of Motorola Startacs? Did I really think that was going to be a good idea? Was I going to be using Motorola Startacs for the next seventy years?"

So she gave in and upgraded. She kept upgrading.

It is such a metaphor for the relationship many of us have with technology.

"When you start to take a long view, you start to realize that, if you don't participate in the current wave of technology, how is the next wave or the wave after that not going to be completely intimidating? It's more important to catch every wave of technology as you are going because it makes it easier to catch the next wave," Mayer said.

I've thought about that story lately. Especially since I have watched so many of my friends get pushed aside, laid off, or outright fired. At first, it was so easy to jump to the conclusion that it was all about age discrimination. But the deeper I dug, I learned that the problem was far more complicated.

Those who weren't born googling in our cribs have been slow to upgrade. We've evolved—a little, but next to someone half our age, most of us are cave people. We've learned about technology, but not nearly enough to make us competitive. We use social media, kind of. We are familiar with artificial intelligence, sort of. But by and large, we haven't caught the waves that keep us out front.

This challenge is just as crucial to a thirty-year-old as it is to someone over fifty.

You might be the best person on earth for your job today and still get canned.

It's just not enough.

Companies are focused on the runway into the future. If you aren't poised to be leading change down the road, you're absolutely getting in line for a whipping. And you probably don't even know it.

If you are on the runway, you are evolving. You see what's coming because you are independently studying the future because it fascinates you. But if you aren't on the runway, if you are just showing up and doing the great job you've always done, you probably haven't noticed that you are not as valuable to your company.

I learned more when I talked to Shelley Broader, former CEO of Chicos FAS and former CEO of a massive international Walmart region. "Some people haven't evolved and stayed current," she said. "They got stuck in a period of time and they just want to put plastic over their sofa because their grandma put plastic over their sofa. That's what I see. There are people who stopped evolving as employers and as employees."

Because of her history in retail, Broader can make this case easily.

"There's been an ongoing battle between brick-and-mortar and digital commerce. The brick-and-mortar people liked stores and hated the digital commerce team because, to them, it was competition. They thought it was going to be a fad. They thought that online sales were going to dilute their store margins. A lot of retailers felt that way, as did a lot of executives.

"All of a sudden, you start looking around and saying, 'That is where my customer is going. I have to change my business to be able to support a lower margin. There are still people in retail in their fifties and sixties who are saying that digital commerce is the worst thing that ever happened to retail and we should have just stayed out of it. They have pegged themselves so hard to an opinion that they can't see the future and they almost feel like they're going to be disloyal to their own genetics if they change their mind about it."

I have a coaching client who has been bypassed for multiple promotions because the company is promoting younger, less experienced people—and paying them more. She is doing a great job. But she is not seen as the face of the future. I helped her come up with an action plan, but she told me she is not comfortable with that. "I'm just going to keep my head down until I retire."

Argh! She doesn't retire for eight years. Eight years is a lifetime in a changing workplace. THERE IS NO KEEPING YOUR HEAD DOWN AND WAITING IT OUT.

If you wish to survive, you must evolve.

Period.

So, your to-do list involves both attitude and action:

1. Accept that change *is*. It just *is*. It is not going to stop.
2. If you are positive about learning and contributing to and advancing change, you will remain a player.
3. Keep reading about trends and discuss what's coming with bosses and coworkers. Get on committees.
4. Visibly evolve. Educate yourself and demonstrate what you are learning.
5. Communicate, communicate, communicate. Show that you exist and are contributing and learning.
6. Ask questions so you know what's coming and how it will affect the company and your job.
7. As you gain expertise, share it with those who haven't kept up so you are visibly part of the change, not the status quo.

Harvard Business Review ran a story that says AI is set to add $13 trillion to the global economy in the next ten years, but implementation is lagging substantially because leadership is having trouble rewiring their organizations.

This technology is here. It's growing. It may not be impacting you today, but believe me, it *will* impact you. Don't be a change resister.

Think of those people who argued with Broader about online shopping.

I received two Amazon packages today. I absolutely have fallen out of the habit of shopping in stores. How about you? My bet is you do much of your shopping online, too, and that trend exploded once we hunkered down for social distancing during the COVID-19 pandemic. So when you think of the people in retail leadership who ignored or mocked online shopping, you can understand why forward-thinking leaders can't stand resisters. They kill businesses because they refuse to move into the unknown.

Imagine the opportunities that exist for you if you are one of the first to adapt and implement.

"It's okay to be really passionate about an opinion and passionate about a direction or cause, and then as you have more life experience and learn and grow with age, you can change that," Broader said. "You don't want to be covert about it and say, 'I was never for that.' It's really refreshing when someone says, 'I used to be against this, but now I understand that point of view and I'm quite bullish about it.' I'm very aware that I'm a different person at fifty-four than I was at forty-four than I was at thirty-four. And I'm sure I'll be a very different person at sixty-four with thoughts and plans and talents."

There is so much emphasis on the workforce of the future. With a gig economy, will people choose to work for one company or have a skill and work for ten companies?

Technology may eliminate your job. It may make it more complicated or even make it easier. It definitely offers tremendous opportunities for those who are quick to evolve.

"I have the ability to know when we launch a new line of clothing, what item sold the most or was even looked at online the most that day," said Broader. "I can know that morning, when it first went out, the first twenty items out of that set sold. I can track everything.

"Our old technology would quickly say, 'These are the winners, buy more of them today.' But artificial intelligence goes way deeper. The old way says, if you sell ten hamburger buns by ten in the morning, that is how busy the store is and you'll probably sell one thousand hamburger buns by the end of the day. But artificial intelligence says that they picked the buns up, looked at them (or clicked on them), but they didn't put them in the cart. Was it price? Packaging? Was it the fact that hamburger was too expensive or there wasn't relish in stock? What was it?"

That information, used right, translates into profit. Why is it that so many more veteran employees have been slow to embrace it?

It sounds complicated. But you learn with time and effort. The more effort, the more you learn. As you learn, you can identify opportunities that play to your strengths.

Somebody still needs to interpret the data.

Maybe nobody can pick or design a garment better than you can, but as far as knowing which garment will sell?

With AI, Broader notes, "You should just say, 'Now my hit rate is going to go up. Instead of designing twenty beautiful things and having two of them work and eighteen not work, now I will have the opportunity to learn and understand a way to maybe get ten to work. We have to get people excited that these tools are not replacements for them."

Your job will become vulnerable if you don't get excited and learn to utilize those tools.

"I am not looking for everyone to be a master of artificial intelligence capabilities," said Ken Burdick, CEO of WellCare. "I want people to be open to the ways in which jobs can be done differently so we can process information differently because of that capability."

But there are other capabilities that matter, too, he said. Little things like wisdom, focus, judgment, leadership, and human communication are also premium skills.

"I see technology as just one dimension, and any group is going to have a whole spectrum of capabilities," he said.

Just be open. Open to anything. Mayer—the leader who loved that Motorola Startac cell phone—learned that the real magic these days is in the unknown. Maybe, as you reshape your career, you will dare to try something that is ill defined and makes no sense. Because much of what is most successful today starts that way and then evolves.

You evolve by letting go of what you expect and are comfortable with. Just dive into something new so you can learn and grow. You can take opportunities that are risky because you have the confidence to know you will land in the right place. But taking advantage of change means understanding that what you expected and experienced earlier in your career is not what will sustain you until the end.

"I joined an eight-person startup that couldn't afford to vacuum the floors," Mayer said. "They didn't have a conference table. I was interviewed at a Ping-Pong table. They sat on exercise balls," she remembered.

Then, she laughed.

"That was Google."

"One of the people they sent in to interview me was employee number eight, who had started two hours earlier. I asked, 'What has it been like to work here?' He said, 'Well, it's been great the two hours that I've been here.'

"I wanted to do something that I felt I wasn't ready to do, and joining an eight-person company that thought it could change the world through search—but wasn't at all clear how, it wasn't at all clear why the world needed another search engine, especially one with a silly name like Google, which I knew could be the brunt of all the family reunion jokes when I was forty. I could just hear my parents and relatives: 'Well, Marissa graduated from Stanford with her 'symbolic systems' degree, then went to a company called—get this—Google.' I learned so much more working at Google, trying to build a great company, that even if we failed, I'd learn more than I would learn succeeding somewhere else."

So she went, she evolved, and then she soared. You can do the same.

4

It's Not Personal

No senior executive will sit for a recorded interview and say, "Oh yeah, we don't like old people here. We don't need or want them. They're slow, they are behind, they're falling apart, and their insurance is too expensive. I'm sick of paying them so much." Nor will any executive say, "Any woman who leaves to take care of her baby for a few years has committed career suicide." No, they all will say that they embrace diversity in the workplace, that the team is always better when people of all ages and backgrounds are represented, and that they have some good older people on their team.

While that is true in some cases, it is not reality for many people. No one is going to lay that truth out there on the table because it'll get them sued.

But I am certainly appreciative of the perspective given by the leaders in this chapter who lay out what you are up against—and why.

Reality at Work

I'm not sure how much of the institutionalized age discrimination was ordained from the top or just manifested itself as tech skills started being more crucial to workplace demands. If you are facing career challenges and are over forty-five (or in many cases, forty), you are not alone. Perhaps you could have prevented trouble by diving deeper and faster into change, but don't flog yourself. This is a common experience and challenge. It's actually quite cliché because *millions* of others are going through the same thing.

Older workers get crapped on.

It's the truth.

One in five workers in the United States is over fifty-five, and according to an AARP study, two out of three of those older workers said age discrimination is an issue at work. When it comes time to find a new job, people over fifty-five need substantially more time to get hired—an average of eight and a half months. That's two and a half months more than younger people, according to the Schwartz Center for Economic Policy Analysis.

It's hard to get work when you are a middle-aged man.

But it's worse when you are a woman.

Add an extra layer of difficulty if you are a minority.

That's just our statistical reality. Younger people are making hiring decisions and are doing what we did when we were young and making hiring decisions: they are picking what and who they know and value. It's apparently a stretch for a thirty-seven-year-old HR manager to say, "This fifty-nine-year-old is exactly what we need!"

Did we do that to older people when we were young? This is not a new issue, but the generational clash with millennials has made it a little more personal and problematic.

There are many reasons we get dissed, and usually it isn't personal.

Sometimes, it really is because you are old and the company, leader, or manager has an "out with the old, in with the new" attitude. Maybe your technical skills can't compete with someone who was playing Nintendo in the womb. Sometimes, the "problem" is that your longevity in your profession has made you expensive.

Newer talent is cheaper. Often it's that, as you age, your salary is higher and your insurance premiums are substantially stiffer.

I know. I've said that already. But when you look at all of those factors together, you have to come to one very important conclusion: IT IS NOT PERSONAL.

Companies have diversity and inclusion groups for sexual orientation, gender, and race, but I have yet to see one on age. I know this because I speak on leadership all over the world for many of the world's largest corporations. I don't think it is an oversight. I imagine that, should they have an initiative to empower professionals of all ages, they'd then have to follow through and attract, train, track, and promote professionals of all ages. Talking about age scares them because it's easier to get away with discriminating in that area, and my bet is that they want to keep that option open.

Yes, there are age-discrimination claims and lawsuits, but victories are very hard fought and rare.

Either Give Up or Buck Up

You can get stuck in that space of wanting justice or revenge, or you can find a more positive route. One route lets you wallow; the other helps you heal.

Stop complaining about the injustice because that does not move you forward. Act to protect your career and come up with new goals and strategies. Yes, there is so much inherent unfairness out there, but that's not going to change in time for you to get the paycheck you need and/or want.

You either give up or buck up.

If this challenge hasn't hit you yet and you are sailing along with no problems, take nothing for granted. You still need to follow the action steps in this book to insulate yourself. Just because you are safe today doesn't mean you will be safe tomorrow or next year or in five years. Change is hitting every industry.

"It is naïve for anybody to not be thinking about the possibility of being sidelined," said Kimberly Ross, the former chief financial officer of Avon, Ahold, and Baker Hughes, who currently serves on several major corporate boards. "I don't care if you are twenty-five or fifty. It almost feels complacent if you don't. Things change in this environment."

The way to create job security is to always act as if you don't have it. Always be in action mode.

After the economic collapse in 2008, companies pared down. Even after the rebound, there was less demand for labor. Combine that with technological change that eliminated the need for certain jobs and the growing force of the millennials who were happy to step in and drive the change that many baby boomers avoided, and the result was opportunity shriveling up on a mass scale right at the time when baby boomers were aging into the last phase of their careers.

"Some of the people doing the hiring started thinking, 'I'm going to go for someone younger because they'll have the energy and they'll be less expensive,'" Ross said. "That is, unless the older employee has a specific, useful skill set."

Pre-COVID-19, the Bureau of Labor Statistics reported that 2.4 million workers forty-five and older were underemployed or unemployed. During COVID-19, the number nearly tripled.

The bias is real, and the perpetrators will likely suffer it when they get older, too.

But there comes a moment when we have to look at ourselves and take a little ownership, too. Unless we realize what sidelined us, we can't fix the problem.

"It's your responsibility to keep your saw sharp," said Regenia Stein, a business consultant and former vice president of business performance, industry development, and communications for

Kraft Foods. "You have to be the one to demonstrate that you are embracing and looking for new responsibility—not waiting to be delegated new responsibility. Show that you are learning new skills, be the first to lead the task force, and be the first one to do the next new thing. Clearly demonstrate that, just because you are tenured, it does not mean you are an old dog who can't learn new tricks."

If you don't do that, she said, there will always be some other hotshot who can do it, who is waiting for you to get out of the way.

Complacency sometimes sets in for those who cling to the old way of thinking that the company will take care of its people until the end, Stein said.

"But that died two decades ago," she said.

You are deluding yourself if you think that what you delivered in the past should count for something. Companies aren't looking at your performance that way.

Your bosses are looking at you as a contributOR. Not someone who contributED, said Karen Stuckey, senior vice president at Walmart.

"Complacency drives elimination," she said. "People feel, rightfully, that they are very unheard. They feel like they've given their loyalty for however many decades and that the company treated them poorly."

But few companies adhere to the old tradition that means seniority equals reward.

"You can't coast, and you're likely going to have to stay in the game longer than many have in the last generation or two," said Ken Burdick, CEO of Centene Corporation and WellCare. "You have to stay relevant longer. Approach it like you are a continuous learner and a student of business. Every industry is evolving. Every profession is evolving. If you don't evolve, you become extinct."

At age sixty, Burdick said he is as excited about what he is doing today as he was thirty-eight years earlier, when he started working in health care. And you can imagine how much his work has changed.

"I've never stopped learning and I've never stopped being open. That is more about mindset than it is about experience and capabilities."

HOW EXPECTATIONS HAVE CHANGED

01 What have you done?

This is what your parents and grandparents had to answer. Experience and past performance mattered. Employers looked at the whole picture of what you'd done to grow into a contributor.

What have you done for me lately? 02

This was what most baby boomers dealt with. Employers wanted you to have a good track record because they wanted consistent delivery. But they also wanted to know you were continuing to deliver.

03 What have you got for tomorrow?

You doubled your numbers? How nice. How about tripling them next quarter? Bosses stopped looking back and focused forward, always raising the bar.

"It doesn't matter if you are the best person for your job today. What about five years from now? 04

Change is so constant that the only people who will thrive in it are those who are constantly educating themselves, upskilling, and strategizing so they are ready to contribute—no matter what.

Do companies care about money more than the people they employ? Good ones care about both. But the financial bottom line is still the bottom line, and that is what stakeholders care about most. Companies are looking far into the future to an environment that is almost unfathomable to most of us.

The Tap on the Shoulder

I mentioned earlier that the idea for this book came over drinks one night at a conference. I was sitting with several senior executives, and as we drank, the truth of their own career challenges started coming out.

One was in her fifties and could not get hired. One had just gotten the push to retire early. Another was being harassed by her CEO, who suddenly felt she could do nothing right. Another was being shoved out from the business she raised up from its infancy.

It does not matter where you are in the hierarchy. It is a fight to stay valued and relevant. But their positions gave them perspective that most of us are not privy to. They illuminated how impersonal the decisions to shake up employee lives can be.

One of the women, a senior vice president at a Fortune 100 company, said she knows the day will come when she gets a quiet tap on the shoulder that signals her time to exit. In more than fifteen years with the company, she has seen many worthy colleagues get "the tap."

"It will start with something like, 'So, let's talk about what your plans are for the next few years.' Or 'We're going to go in a different direction and that will start tomorrow and thank you.' And they'll be effusive about everything you've done for the company, but the outcome is the same. I have really mentally started to prepare myself to depersonalize it.

"The organization is always on to the next. You really can't tie your sense of worth to what a company does or doesn't do to or with you."

Isn't that age discrimination?

"It flat-out is age discrimination, but discrimination is usually with intent," she said. "I think it's just age oblivion. I don't really think an organization intends to discriminate against their older associates."

Corporations are looking at money.

"A lot of these decisions have to do with cost, and so it's efficiency," Stein said. "It's a combination of always wanting the newest shiny object and it's also this notion of a more cost-effective workforce. As someone gets to be at the top of their game, they're also quite expensive. When you consider new talent or new initiative, along with cost, they make changes."

Nothing personal. It's money. It's shiny objects. It's happening every day to many, many people, so it is not you.

The Financial Hit

Executives generally have nice, soft landings when they are pushed out. They get a package. They've been paid a lot over the years, and few will ever worry that the financial implications will drag them under. Not so for the average American worker, who is lucky to get any severance at all. Their exits are often sudden, brutal, and unnecessarily cruel.

It doesn't just hit their pride. It hits their ability to put food on the table.

The Economic Policy Institute issued a report on what households led by people in their fifties have socked away for retirement. For those between fifty and fifty-five, it's an average of $124,831. The people between fifty-six and sixty-one have saved $163,577. But that is the average, and that's skewed by the people who have put a ton of money away. The report said the median retirement savings is just $8,000 for people in their early fifties and $17,000 for people in their late fifties.

Yikes.

A different study by the Transamerica Center for Retirement Studies said 59 percent of fiftysomething employees are counting on working past age sixty-five or not retiring at all because they won't have the money.

It's not like employment is optional because we hit a certain age. Most people are doing the best they can and can't easily rebound from a sudden firing. It forces them into absolute desperation.

Maybe it is not personal, but why does it have to be so heartless?

I was also saddened during a conversation with Anita Burrell, who faced the realization that bad things can happen, whether you are delivering or not, or whether you are doing altruistic work like developing lifesaving drugs at different pharmaceutical companies.

"I realized I was not important," she said. "We live in a life-and-death industry. But sometimes it feels like nobody cares about your life or your career death. Most of us went into the industry to help the patients and, while I think big companies care about patients, individuals are not as central as you'd like to think they are." She named two pharmaceutical corporations that had both laid off hundreds of people that week.

There is so much turmoil in that industry that she's felt the impersonal knife in the back more than once. Every time, she's gotten back up. As she and her colleagues age, the constant starting over does get a little wearisome.

My hairdresser—who should be writing self-help books for the rest of us—escaped Vietnam in a boat where people were literally stacked on top of each other for two weeks. People died on the journey. Her story is horrific, but her resilience is inspiring. We talked about what happens in aging and she explained it so simply: "For many years, God gave and gave and gave to us," she said. "Money, career, health. Now God slowly takes things back."

Whoa.

It does feel like there is a bit of subtraction going on in our workplaces. But I have to wonder what qualities define those who fight back and win at this point in life? Certainly, there are many people whose fortitude leads to more success despite bias and discrimination.

You might try, try, try and still experience a professional defeat that challenges your finances and viability. More than anything, that experience challenges your self-worth. You have a lifetime of knowledge and wisdom—more than you have ever had—yet suddenly it isn't valued.

You feel as if *you* aren't valued, and that is crushing. It also is terribly unfair and downright insulting, especially if the people who judge and reject you are far less knowledgeable or experienced.

There's not much to say about it but this: those who treat you poorly are getting older by the minute. Their turn is coming, too, and karma's a bitch.

And again: it's not personal. That doesn't help your finances or your future, but it does soothe the ego a bit to understand that there are literally millions of people experiencing the same thing.

What I don't get is this: if leaders are worried about who is going to drive the future in five years, why are they counting on people who might not be there? It's not the boomers and Gen Xers who are going to abandon them. They aren't continuous job jumpers.

A Deloitte study reported that 43 percent of millennials expect to leave their jobs within two years, and just 28 percent want to stay longer than five. Gen Z workers are even less likely to stay put, with 61 percent planning to stay less than two years and only 12 percent planning to hang out more than five.

Companies are banking on people who aren't banking on them.

Makes little sense, but that's what they are doing.

Be Proactive, Not Reactive

So that fact that young workers have high turnover rates sure looks like a window of opportunity to me. If you can rebrand yourself as a go-to contributor who will stay, you'll add value AND staying power. You have to demonstrate that you are well above the stereotype of an older worker and show that you'll be there to deliver.

"You need to declare your interest in moving forward," said Tom Greco, CEO of Advance Auto Parts and former CEO of Frito-Lay. "Some people don't do that until there is a problem. Be proactive."

No more holding your breath and hoping things will work out. Do that and things probably won't.

"You have to be proactive, not reactive, and take charge of your life," said Helayne Angelus, cofounder of the global group LEAD, Leading Executives Advancing Diversity. "What are you doing to continually challenge yourself and grow? Do you understand the digital revolution? Do you spend your time in your own little world with people just like you? Do you volunteer with diverse groups? Do you spend time with people who are younger, and do you understand how they think and where they are coming from? There is a lot of ownership in this because every day you have to prove your value—wherever you are."

Angelus, the former VP of customer development for Procter & Gamble, has been a great mentor to me. She can boil anything down to the bullet points that matter, so I asked her to coach you. Here's what she came up with:

1. Know thyself. That has to be the most important thing. If you don't know yourself really well, you are going to be completely blindsided. Do the hard work. Create your own personal mission statement and review. What are you really good at? What makes you happy? What are your unique, value-added skills? What are your flat spots that you're not good at? Find ways to leverage what you are great at while minimizing your flat spots by utilizing the diverse people around you.

2. Every day, do something that scares you. Get out of your comfort zone. Do what makes you uncomfortable. If you are doing the same kinds of things with the same people in the same places, the chances of you being personally disrupted in an organization will be high.

3. Be a lifelong learner. Do you understand what future trends are? There is no excuse not to be a lifelong learner today. There are a million TED Talks and YouTube videos available that require you to learn new things and talk about them.

This is a tough reality, but remember: some people are still winning.

Do you have another fight left inside of you?

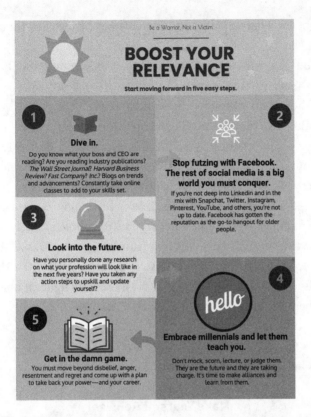

Computer learning is an amazing resource, but one of the most powerful resources—as noted by virtually every leader I interviewed—is other people.

"Don't be afraid to ask for help—ever," said Jill Smart, president of the National Academy of Human Resources and the former chief human resources officer for Accenture, which has more than 450,000 employees. "Remember, you don't get what you don't ask for."

If you don't know where to start, well, "*That's* where you ask for help," said Smart. "If the issue is that you haven't kept up with tech, take a class. If you can't relate well to millennials, find some millennials who will help you. Interact with them and get

insight on what you can do differently to better gain their respect."

You can win with these dynamics, said Crate and Barrel
CEO Neela Montgomery.

"There is no reason for the world to pass you by on this stuff,"
she said. "Not everybody will end up being a programmer. There
will be plenty of roles and jobs. But you have to do the learning yourself. If you wait for the company to educate you and en-
hance your skills, well, that is not workable. There is so much
learning available now in computers. Technologies have posi-
tives and negatives, right. You can upskill yourself on any topic
at any time and, usually, it is free. Think more, read more about
how your role in the industry is changing. People often think
that is a leadership question, that the leader will figure it out and
tell them the answer. That is no longer the case."

And there you have it.

It's on you.

What a tremendous opportunity.

Make Yourself Relevant

I would love to be able to tell you that there are seven easy steps
for you to take and that within thirty days you will be relevant
and more in demand than ever in your career. This is not a step-
by-step situation. This is a process that begins and ends with a
decision on your part to stop judging your obstacles and start figuring them out. At some point, there is a come-to-Jesus moment
when you have to acknowledge that you have some ownership in
this.

Of course, you don't want to read that. Who does? Who really wants to know that by tuning out or tiptoeing into change
they missed the bus?

It is time to look in the mirror and be honest about what's going on here.

1. **Are you your greatest asset or obstacle?** Have you been keeping up? Have you been criticizing change, change agents, or younger people? Have you been scoffing at or hiding from the widespread use of social media?

2. **Catch your breath.** Even if you are responsible for some of the obstacles you are currently facing, don't beat yourself up. You have millions of peers who have done the same thing. What differentiates you is that you are going to make the decision to climb out of this.

3. **Make the decision.** If you can wholeheartedly decide that you will do whatever it takes to become relevant and follow through with commitment and action, you will have a viable career. Decide, commit, and you are suddenly leaping ahead of the others who are still angry or mystified that their careers have stalled out.

4. **Start reading business- or industry-related articles for an hour every day.** Before you can decide where you are going, you need to find out where your industry is going. That means you need to start reading new publications and consume information about trends with artificial intelligence, robotics, big data, blockchain, the "workplace of the future," whatever. Learn the resources that are going to predict what is ahead for your industry.

5. **Stop commiserating.** This is, indeed, a tremendous challenge. But the frustrations of others will sap your hope and do nothing to set you on the right course.

If the people you are talking with are not helping you refocus and redirect, find people who will. Come up with a cabinet of people who are in your industry, people who know you well, people who are younger and older, and people who will have your back as you move forward in this challenge.

6. **Sign up for your first online class.** Begin upskilling immediately, learning something you should know but don't. If that's too daunting, start with a twenty-minute YouTube video. If you don't know how to use LinkedIn, take a ten-minute LinkedIn tutorial. If you need to know the basics of artificial intelligence, find a video about that. Start to expand your mind slowly so you get the basics.

7. **Start talking to other people.** Process what you are reading and learning by speaking with others, which will start you on the path toward innovative thinking and applying what you are learning to your industry. You are now a forward thinker, so you need to have opportunities to brainstorm forward-thinking thoughts. Instead of talking about the usual old stuff, start brainstorming with others about what the future is going to look like.

8. **Get serious about guerilla networking.** Who you know will drive so much of your success. Find ways to meet, befriend, and brainstorm with the people you need to know. Stay in contact! Ask for advice. Share dog or kid stories, but connect on a personal level and build a network that is going to help you find the opportunities that you can't find on your own.

9. **Develop a list of goals for each month.** Set deadlines. If you need to learn five things about technology or workplace trends, plot them out on a calendar. Figure out what you need to know and set deadlines. Then, know

what you're going to do to apply some of that knowledge and let others know that you have it. As you add new skills to your repertoire, constantly update your résumé.

10. **Lighten up.** Once you are on this path, you are on the path. You can have full confidence that this will work. So stop obsessing about money and obstacles and potential failures. Just learn to enjoy the learning and growth you are experiencing with certainty that it will lead you to something that will create more success. You may be in uncomfortable territory, but learn to enjoy it. It's not going to get easier, but you are doing something that few are doing, and so you can walk with confidence, knowing you will be successful.

11. **Just put one foot in front of the other.** That's all you can do, and it will work. If you just take one step and then another, you will get where you need to go.

Accept, Cope, and Adapt

I've referred to my core coping strategy as: "accept, cope, and adapt." I learned this when my mother first started showing signs of Alzheimer's disease, and it is my mantra whenever things get rough. When Mom would repeat the same thing a hundred times, I focused on the wonder of the sound of her voice because I knew the day was coming when she would not be able to talk at all. So, the faster I learned to accept, cope, and adapt, the faster I could enjoy what I still had of my mother, instead of what I'd lost. When she couldn't communicate at all, I just treasured holding her because she was still alive. Sure, there were dark moments, but I got through them quickly during her twelve-year ordeal.

What an incredible lesson! It is on us to face life and get on with things. The faster we do it, the faster we feel better.

It's your choice whether or not you wallow in your difficulties if you are being forced to reinvent. The faster you accept, cope, and adapt, the faster you are on your way to succeeding. Every time you start to doubt yourself, just send the negative thought away and say, "I *know* I am going to win." The more you say it, the more you know it.

You're going to have to do something, right? So do it with gusto. Dive in and make it an adventure. All you have to do is accept, cope, and adapt.

5

Identity in Crisis

It's easy to flatline emotionally when your career is in free fall.

Emotional exhaustion is a given. The uncertainty is depleting. Your self-esteem is challenged daily. And yet, in the moments when you are feeling your worst about yourself, you must rally and project your best.

If you lose faith in yourself, who is going to have faith in you?

A comeback demands movement, *some movement*, every day. And yet, when you feel bad about yourself, it can be a challenge to move at all. You must do something to continually move yourself toward your goal, and doing that means braving the one thing that your sad paralysis tries to prevent: you've got to put yourself out there and decide to win.

The good thing about bad times is that they are the best moments to go deep, take stock, and fortify your identity.

When you start facing career challenges, it is common to experience a painful loss of identity. If you aren't the successful professional you once were, who are you? A loser?

Of course not.

You are still the same successful person you always were—with a new challenge. These challenges do not negate all your previous work and success.

An identity crisis lets you define who you are on a soul level, sans title. Your work may have made you great or made great things happen, but who you are on a spiritual and emotional level is really what you have and will become in this life. While everything else is in chaos, you can find great calm in this new experience of being personally inspired while professionally challenged.

Who are you?

You are not your job. You never were.

You have the choice to wallow in your misfortune or find the deeper, human identity that will stay with you until the day you die.

We have many identities: partner, spouse, grandparent, professional, activist, gardener, adventurer, spiritual being, enforcer, rule breaker . . . so many different facets of every individual. That is who you are to yourself and the world.

Sadly, people often process tough professional challenges as an assault on their inner identity. You can allow that or push back. Rejection stings. But the things you are being criticized or rejected for are probably things that are utterly meaningless in the bigger picture of life. God or the universe or whatever you believe is in charge does not care about any of that. What matters is that you grow as a good human being.

I find strength and inspiration from the "famous failures" that made unbelievable comebacks. Elvis got a C in high school music class and was told he couldn't sing. Walt Disney was fired from a newspaper because he "lacked imagination" and "had no original ideas." Lucille Ball was told to leave New York and give up on acting because she had "no talent." Warren Buffett was rejected for admission to the Harvard Business School. J. K. Rowling was a welfare mom. And Oprah Winfrey was demoted from her job as a TV anchorwoman and told she was "not fit for television." This list goes on and on.

Those superstars prevailed because they took their knocks and fought back. They did not let others define them. They defined themselves.

Don't let adversity define you. It's just a set of obstacles. What matters is what you do with them.

The Show Isn't Over

You may catch yourself shrinking emotionally because you and your circumstances are filling your psyche with doubt. You react that way initially because much of this experience feels unexpected and undeserved. But the one thing you can control is your individual resolve and resilience.

The show isn't over. You are as good as you ever were. You are an accomplished person who deserves a great life. I think we are here on this earth to define who we are on a human level—not a professional level. So who are you going to be? A warrior or a wimp? This is the one part of your challenge that is all on you. Who are you going to be now that you are facing these big obstacles?

Identity is not about professional achievements or accolades. It is about values and connections. It is about why you live on this earth.

What really centers you? For me, it is fresh air in the great outdoors. No matter what else is going on in my life, I can dive into nature in a deeply personal, life-affirming way. What does that for you? Does nature give you a boost? Or is it your relationships? Experiences? Exercise? Travel? Whatever excites you is where you should turn to find fulfillment and purpose as you work through your career issues. You have to lift yourself up so you are at your best.

Understanding Dark Times

There will be dark moments, but dark valleys are where our greatest growth happens. You may lose your sense of purpose—or find it. That is your choice.

Life becomes much easier once you stop seeking fairness or order. Your life challenges are growing you into a person who will either choose to be strong or weak, agile or frozen.

So if you are wondering who you are and doubting whether you are any good, rest assured. You are as magnificent as you want to be. You just need to know in your soul that you are whole—no matter what. Nobody can take your soul identity from you, but you certainly have the ability to throw it away.

You can often help fix what feels threatened or small on the inside by fortifying yourself on the outside. Volunteer to help others. Take classes in something you've never tried, and become proficient in something unrelated. Make new friends. Exercise. Lean on your family and loved ones. Lean on your spirituality.

Stop Catastrophic Thinking

Your mind will make you as crazy as you let it. Learn to recognize when you have slipped into "catastrophic thinking" mode and fight back.

If you are out of work and not finding a job, your mind might put you in this loop: "I'm spending my savings. I am going to run out of money. I didn't get that job. I'll never get any job. I can make it three more months on my savings. Then I'll have to sell my house. Where will I stay? How will I feed my family? Will we be homeless? I'm going through my savings. I'm not getting a job. I'll probably have to go work at Walmart—will Walmart hire me? I can't live on that money. I can't feed my family. We will be homeless . . ."

Your brain is more than willing to let you turn an ordinary

challenge into a catastrophe. You have to take charge and control your perspective.

Replace catastrophic thoughts with more realistic thoughts.

Train your mind to say, "Well, this is tough, but I'll find a way. I'm not going to blow this out of proportion. I've got great support. I believe in myself. I've succeeded in the past and I will succeed in the future. This is hard, but I'll get through it. I'm going to win. I will find a way."

Once you take charge of your perspective, the catastrophe will shrink back into a challenge. You'll find your way through this.

The odds of your being unable to find your way through your current challenge and having to eat out of a garbage pail are zero.

Zero.

I shouldn't have to tell you that, but that thought (or something similarly ridiculous) is not uncommon when people are forced to start over or reinvent in middle age and beyond. Self-doubt feeds on itself and you lose perspective, which makes you lose hope.

When you give up, others aren't victimizing you. You are victimizing yourself.

Maintain Perspective

You are one of 7,442,000,000 people on this earth. Despite your challenges, your problems are not the worst ones in the world. They are not the worst in the United States or the worst in your city. They are likely not the worst in your neighborhood or even on your street.

So make up your mind to buck up and carry on.

You may beat yourself up because you didn't see this situation coming or could have done more to prevent it. You may dive so far into self-doubt that you wonder if you ever deserved any of the success you had. You may tell yourself that it's all downhill from here. You may kick yourself for not saving more or failing to network better. You may think that others are laughing at you. Or you may be really, really mad.

But how are any of those thoughts helping you?

We've been told our whole lives that there is a power in positive thinking, but when we are struggling, it's pretty hard to take charge of our thoughts. Instead, our negative thoughts attract more negative thoughts until the only thoughts we have are negative. The world becomes a dark, ugly place as we are consumed by despair.

Your brain will do a number on you if you let it. You can slide into a negative loop that will tell you that you are a worthless, stupid, overweight loser because, for some reason, the brain will let you get away with that kind of endless self-mutilation.

When you tell yourself such things, is it any wonder that your mind responds by manifesting more negativity and adversity for you? If you put that out there, who on earth will want to bet on you? Instead of saying, "Nobody wants me; I must suck," start saying, "I believe in myself. It'll all work out."

And say, "What if my greatest success is still ahead of me? I'm not done!"

Then say it again. And again. And again and again and again.

Attack Worry and Stress

If a problem is fixable, if a situation is such that you can do something about it, then there is no need to worry. If it's not fixable, then there is no help in worrying. There is no benefit in worrying whatsoever.

—Dalai Lama XIV

That Dalai Lama quote is the best.

But His Holiness was never unemployed. He was never

disregarded because of his age or his looks. And people seem to like him more the older he gets.

I know you are worried right now because we're all worried. I think of Linda Cruz, who had a stellar career in the pharmaceutical industry before going through one crucible moment after another until she finally got a job where she was making less than a third of what she once made. "You know what you can do, but nobody wants you anymore. It is very lonely. They don't value what you have," she told me.

Painful.

Chuck Leonard said he felt humiliated for the last two years of his job as an analyst in the insurance industry, knowing he wasn't wanted there and certain he would be fired, which he finally was.

"It was humiliating on every level," he said. "For two years, I was demoralized. Then I had no job, no insurance, no dignity, no hope. I felt like I had failed everybody, and I couldn't get an interview—no matter how many jobs I applied for. It took me nine months, the longest nine months of my life. I had one company that interviewed me four times, and I thank God they hired me. I'm so grateful."

When you are being pulled under by a nearly crippling brush with adversity, self-help tips and suggestions on managing worry may fall flat. Once you are in a tailspin, everything seems to suffer. When work goes south, it can hit your finances hard, and that impacts relationships. Your self-esteem gets a body slam, and often health is compromised. Are you worrying about your bills? Your relationship? The past? How you'll ever get your career right? Getting older? Rejection? Are you worrying about what other people think? About what might go wrong? Are you struggling because you have no control?

How do you put worry in its place when life is out of control?

Gratitude, gratitude, gratitude. Gratitude can stop a negative spiral. You have so much to be thankful for. Whenever you doubt that, imagine living in a war-torn country in fear for your life. Knowing you are blessed can minimize stress and worry over what isn't going right for you.

Be mindful. ONLY focus on right now.

Do affirmations. Science backs me up on this. If you repeat an affirmation enough times, your brain will believe it. So . . .

I think only positive thoughts.

I am confident and strong.

I am filled with energy, hope, and joy. I am excited about my future.

I am so optimistic about the future that my stress has disappeared.

I have so much talent and am proud of my success. I'm just getting started.

I live in the moment and only think about what is happening TODAY.

One foot in front of the other, I will get where I need to go.

Everything will work out.

I'm getting a great new opportunity.

This is only a temporary setback.

As long as I remain positive, I can do anything I set my mind to doing.

Say your affirmations twenty-five times a day the first two weeks and then ten times a day the second two weeks, and you will see results.

Exercise. Research has found that exercise boosts your alertness, concentration, and cognitive function while reducing fatigue. Physical activity produces endorphins, our body's "natural painkillers," and they help us sleep, which definitely cuts stress. Your health will improve (healthy body, healthy mind), and your anxiety will diminish.

Read good fiction. It's hard to worry if you get lost in a good book because the brain tends to go to one place or the other. If you are too set on worrying, you will have to keep rereading paragraphs. So find some great escape fiction and use that to create a worry break.

Volunteer. When you feel useless, go be of use! Volunteer. When you help others, you feel better about yourself. The negatives in your head get quieter. It feels good to know that you matter and that you are contributing to a purpose.

List your steps. If you are facing a significant life overhaul, write out your to-do list so you don't freeze because of the enormity of what's ahead. It's much easier to just check off your tasks, one at a time. I always tell young people that if they need to go back to school, break it up into steps: apply, register, take a course, and then another and another. Use this same technique as you plan your way through your current situation. What is your major goal? What are the small steps that will get you there? Take things one at a time, and you will find your way.

Do one thing. This goes along with the last one, but it is different because a long list of steps can be overwhelming on its own. So, when you feel stuck, do one thing that gives you momentum toward fixing your situation. Even if there are ten things you must do, focusing on one is doable. Instead of focusing on ten problems, pick one. You may need to focus on all ten, but that is impossible. Better to accomplish something than to paralyze yourself with fear.

Stop Complaining, Especially with Others

Misery loves company, but it also makes miserable people more miserable.

The fastest way to head into a downward spiral is to start commiserating with someone else. They may validate you. But their misery does not make you feel better. It just makes you feel less alone.

There are endless sad posts of people commiserating online about what is no longer working in their careers, how poorly they are being treated, how they can't find employment anywhere, and how they can't catch a break. I promise you: read that stuff for ten minutes and you are going to feel depressed. The brain is pretty good at listening to what you tell it. Fill it with negativity and it thinks negatively. Fill it with positivity and it thinks positively.

When things get rough, it's hard to go all-out Pollyanna, but you can take steps to keep yourself from sliding into the depths. You are responsible for the filter in your brain. The more you let yourself commiserate or wallow, the darker things will seem. Don't talk about your situation endlessly and don't let others wallow, either. Don't continuously tell "the story." If you have a friend who is going through the same thing, decide whether you can help keep each other on track and feeling better or whether you are bringing each other down.

Sliding into Depression

It is only natural to get the blues and go a little dark when bad things start to happen, but you can usually control how dark you let it get.

Few situations are black and white, but once you become toxically negative in your brain, they sure seem that way. Since you don't feel there is abundant hope, you may assume there is no hope at all. If you haven't succeeded lately, you may tell yourself you are a failure. If one person is critical of something you've done, you may assume their perception of you is worse than it really is, and then you take another leap and assume that most or all people share that same twisted perception.

If you are clinically depressed, get treatment! There is no shame in this and there are effective treatments, whether therapeutic or prescribed medication. Don't self-medicate with alcohol, drugs, or food; doing so will derail your comeback.

Always take time and give yourself a break. Five minutes where you are not allowed to think one negative thought. Tell yourself this: *It's going to be okay. I'm fine. I deserve good things. I believe in myself. I can be happy. I'm feeling happier right now. I feel stronger right now.*

Repeat.

And repeat again.

It's a start.

Never Surrender

It's up to you. Do you think you are denied new, great success because of your age, because you have taken an extended time-out, because you have endured more rejections than you have the stomach to handle? You may not be able to hike the same, familiar path you were hiking, but you are smart enough to pick up and redefine. You aren't done.

The obstacles you face are not unique to you. We know that. But we also know that a certain percentage of people do come back after extended gaps for parenting or travel or caregiving. A certain percentage do stay viable and employed until they reach retirement age—and beyond. If some people can do it, why not you? There is always opportunity out there. It's just not easy opportunity.

No, you aren't enjoying this. But have you *ever* enjoyed those painful moments when someone or something has forced you to pick yourself up and figure out what the hell you are going to do with the rest of your life? What did you do then?

You have to be stronger, smarter, faster, and better than you were when you were half your age, but you can do this.

YOU. ARE. NOT. DONE.

And, look. By now, some of your friends have been hit by a terrible health crisis. One minute, all was well with them. And then it wasn't. It was suddenly horrific. They didn't get a warning notice that they'd better take an extra-long run and eat twice at the buffet because life as they knew it was about to change forever.

It just changed forever.

In an instant.

It's a reminder that you can be minding your own business today or tomorrow or the next day and *ZAP!* A doctor is telling you that you have cancer or a heart condition or signs of dementia.

So even if you are staring down some serious career challenges, do not forget what you've got. You've got your life. And while you sort out what you are going to do next, don't forget to live it. You don't know how much time you have to do fun stuff, so it's your choice how you use what time you've got—or not.

Living mindfully, in the moment, is one of the greatest stress reducers there is. It is something you have to consciously learn to do. But once you get it, you let go of all your what-ifs and just breathe in what you've got. Sunshine on your face. Trees blowing in the wind. A loved one at your side. You dog waiting to show you that you really are the most important person in the world.

The minute you learn to take charge of your worries, you begin to live.

6

How to Catch Up

Waaaaay back in the late 1900s, you know, the previous century, our big boss held a meeting to tell us we were getting new computer equipment to connect us to the "information superhighway." Other bosses kept talking about the information superhighway and how we'd need to use it for our work in the newsroom. The new computers arrived, and I didn't know what was on the superhighway or how to use it because I missed the training while on vacation. I saw many of my fellow reporters using the computers, but I was clueless about what they were doing and too afraid to ask for help.

This went on for a few weeks. Every day, I'd see more people using the information superhighway, and I knew that, every day, I was falling further behind. I was drowning in fear, totally intimidated by this revolutionary new technology.

One day, my coworker, Karen Abbott, came back from the information superhighway machine and I blurted, "I don't know how to use the information superhighway. I don't know what to do."

She smiled.

"Come with me," she said.

She sat at the terminal, called up a search engine, picked a topic, then clicked on one of the results.

"There," she said. "Now you know everything you need to know about using the information superhighway."

It took less than two minutes. Suddenly, all my stress vanished.

The information superhighway was, of course, the Internet.

I had imagined that it would be impossible to get caught up, but it was no big deal.

And so I say to you, if you feel behind, like you are clueless on what you need to know, like you will never get it, just come with me.

Have a seat.

This is not that hard!

You may have a lot to learn, but there are so many easy ways to learn it that all you have to do is make up your mind, open up your mind, then put your mind to work.

It may seem like this will be so time consuming, you will have to sacrifice your whole life just to get caught up. Not true. You'll have to read and study and test and try, but you don't have to read every word. All you have to do is start learning and focus intensely for a couple of months.

Here is some good news: if you are taking extra courses, you are taking them to learn and expand your credentials. You don't have to get perfect scores. You don't need straight As. If you are reading, you don't have to read every word of every article. You are about to go on a mission of learning and upskilling that will be as exciting and stimulating as you allow it to be.

Read, Watch, and Talk

If you are reading the right publications, checking in with the right social media groups, and staying up on what's going on in your trade and professional journals, you will quickly see what it is that you need to study in depth.

The Internet makes it so easy to distract ourselves and give our time away to the most inane or useless time vampires. For now, you have to get more serious about what you are reading. It can still be interesting and entertaining, but it's time to start reading with purpose.

Basic reads. At a minimum, add *The Wall Street Journal, Harvard Business Review,* and *Fast Company* to your daily reading. You don't have to read every article. Scan the headlines for stories that may be relevant to your needs. Read the summaries. If they seem necessary, read the whole story. Or half of it. You are aiming to get more current, and this is really fun reading. It gives you things to talk about with your colleagues and friends, and when you talk about them, you demonstrate that you are keeping abreast of what is going on.

Trade reads. Some people love reading trade journals and scouring their industry websites. Some can't get enough of what their associations are putting out there. I am not one of those people, but I have learned that I have to do a certain amount of this because I can't be viable if I don't know what is up.

Social reads. Find three LinkedIn groups and follow five useful Twitter feeds that will keep you posted on the latest and be engaged with the people who are talking about these developments. It's a start.

Podcasts. Which ones are relevant to your industry? There are more than fifty-four million podcast episodes for you right now, on just about every subject you can imagine. Start listening when you are exercising or commuting.

Employment ads. Scan them not only for your current level of employment but one or two levels higher. These ads will tell you exactly what employers want of the people they are going to bring in and advance.

Watch TED. Make TED and TEDx Talks a regular part of

your entertainment menu. They give you current, fresh ideas. They teach you things you never thought about. And they give you something interesting to talk about!

Talk to everyone. If you want to learn the latest, talk to leaders and developers where you work. Or talk to the young people who seem to have everything mastered. Talk to your kids and their friends. Listen to what others are learning, and you will learn.

Which Topics?

Since there are a million things to study, start reading on trends and see where your greatest deficiencies are. Then start with one topic. Definitely get caught up on AI, robotics, blockchain, big data, machine learning, and all of that. And innovation. You don't have to be so proficient you can program everything. You just need to know what they are, what they do, and how they impact your profession and job.

Pick **three areas** for intense study. Study all three, but try to master one every month so you can add something else to the list.

Then, get started.

Don't make yourself miserable doing this. It's all about attitude. If you have to take a break from bingeing on Netflix or watching animal videos on Facebook, do it. If you really look at how much time you have every day, odds are, there is at least an hour that you are blowing on stupid stuff. Take a two-month hiatus from Facebook. It will not kill you. Use that extra hour to read, read, read so you know what it is you need to study in depth.

Go to Harvard. Or Columbia. Or Wharton.
(A) You Can and (B) It's Free

I've studied innovation via MIT; business leadership through the University of California, Berkeley; and artificial intelligence through Columbia.

Impressed? I'm so glad. But, it actually is no big deal.

You can do the same thing, free, with a few weeks of minimal effort.

The place you should start is edx.org or coursera.org, the two biggest MOOCs. MOOCs are "Massive Open Online Courses." The biggies are Coursera, edX, FutureLearn, Cognitive Class, and Udacity. And there are others. Many, many, many others.

Lucky us.

You can upskill quickly by taking online courses led by faculty members at premier institutions from around the world. Most of them are FREE to audit.

Imagine what your employer or potential employer will think when you show that you have updated your skill set with courses from Harvard. Or MIT. Or Columbia, Berkeley, or even the University of Oxford. What if you have completed coursework on tech issues led by Microsoft and IBM? With that kind of coursework on your résumé, you sound current, knowledgeable, and totally promotable and hirable. It does *not* mean you are a Harvard graduate. But it means you are on your game.

These courses are designed to reach working people—not only college students. They have engaging video programs, and the readings are, for the most part, easy to grasp. But the best part of the classes is that they are so well organized and summarize the latest research on whatever topic you want to study.

I have only experienced one dud, but I just deleted the registration from my queue and it vanished. No withdrawal penalty.

The course descriptions say these classes take four, six, or ten weeks, but you can focus and get a class done in a few days if you apply yourself. It's pass/fail. You are auditing the class, so all pressure is off for grades and papers. When you finish, you absolutely know what you need to know on that topic.

It's not as though someone who takes a four-week online

class "went to Harvard," but you can certainly list all of this impressive coursework on your résumé, and that looks AMAZING when you are trying to differentiate yourself.

While most of these courses are free to audit, you can pay a very reasonable amount (most seem to be $50–$250) for a "certificate" to prove you did it. It is not likely that anyone would ask for the certificate, so just take these courses to get your brain back in the game.

I enjoyed a comprehensive business leadership course from UC Berkeley on the foundations of happiness at work. It brought together the latest research on how to take the "soft" skills of leadership (where you actually treat your people like human beings) and turn them into practice in leadership. They had videos of interviews or presentations with major business leaders, and the faculty was very engaging. By the time I finished, I felt I knew enough to go to different companies and present keynotes on the issue. It was that good. And, again, it was free. It took about twenty hours of my time.

My current plan is to take the following courses: Artificial Intelligence, Blockchain for Business, The Future of Work (Preparing for Disruption), and Corporate Innovation. Imagine how those classes will teach and broaden me. And studying through prestigious schools will definitely make me relevant and prepared.

You need to constantly expand your skills. You can take the courses from a range of institutions, adding prestige to your résumé. These programs are well worth the time because you get a little designer label to add to your résumé, even if you did not complete a degree there. Many recruiters know that these are free classes, but they also know that some of them are challenging and intense.

I recently finished a class through MIT that taught me about user innovation and entrepreneurship. I learned how to dig into my own life to find ideas to innovate, then make decisions about how to develop and market them. By the time I was done with the class, I had a good idea and a plan to advance it. Even if I never pursue that idea, the class showed me how simple it is to find inspiration when we think we have none.

It was fun learning because the course used informative videos to back up the concepts. Being that the class was pass/fail, there was zero pressure. I could sit on my couch and learn from one of the nation's premier academics on the innovation process. And let me tell you: WOW. It taught me where to come up with ideas, how to flesh them out, and where to find the people to put them to use. If I need another career, I will use this class to develop a winning idea!

There is so much to learn, but IT IS NOT HARD TO DO IT!

The beauty of advancing your education at this point in your career is that you already have an education. You don't need to go and get another degree—you just need to know the information. That means you don't have the pressure of getting a good grade or writing long papers trying to impress the instructor. I don't care if the instructor even knows I am alive. I just want to get through the coursework so I can fill my knowledge gaps.

The statistics of online learning suggest millions of people *love* the idea, but they stop short of doing the work. Udemy reported that 4 percent of the people who sign up for online classes actually finish them. Seventy percent sign up and never even begin the program. And of those who start, most bail after they have done about 30 percent of the work.

And?

Really, if you at least start it, you are taking a step toward the knowledge you need to be more viable in the workplace.

YouTube videos are useful for quick introductions to topics, but the quality is uneven. I prefer the programs put out by respected, accredited colleges, universities, and tech behemoths because you are getting the latest information and a productive immersion in the topic.

Balance out your studies so you get some tech, but also some leadership skills (which might help you decipher what is really going on in the workplace), project management, data management, trends, and more. At a minimum, you are going to want to learn about social media marketing, career marketing (via LinkedIn), artificial intelligence, blockchain, robotics, and the workplace of the future.

So if you want to start helping yourself, commit to doing one class a month. In a year, it'll be as if you had a whole new college degree in what is current in the world, and being current is career currency.

Start Advertising Your Relevance

Once you are doing your reading and taking your courses, start advertising what you are learning and thinking on social media or in other forums. That way, you are presenting yourself as an expert with in-demand qualifications. Best of all, the advertising is free and reaches people who can advance your career.

Be creative about leveraging your network. You don't just want people passing your résumé around or saying nice things about you. If you know someone who is on the committee for your industry's annual conference, find out if you can make your way onto a panel or do a presentation. That positions you as current, relevant, *and* a visible leader.

Write articles for your industry's magazines or website! They are always looking for free content, and every time you get a byline, that is free advertising.

Do a TEDx Talk! A TEDx slot can be difficult to get, but it is very doable. TEDx lists all the upcoming events. Pick one or two that are at least six or eight months in the future, and go through the application process to create a talk. It is easier to arrange a TEDx in a smaller town, but the recordings still look great and all go on the same TEDx website. The big differentiator is your fresh, new idea. And you will have a lot of them because you are reading and studying and learning. Doing a TEDx is valuable because the recordings are professionally done and just about everybody is impressed by them. Plus, the process is very enjoyable. You meet new people, force yourself to stretch new muscles, and put together ideas and concepts that show you are thinking, focusing, and delivering.

It Won't Take Forever

I know it is easy to feel like you will never catch up, but you will. It will not take years. It may take weeks or, more likely, months. But what an exciting thing to do. Dive in and, step by step, reclaim your power and make yourself current and much more hirable.

The good thing about diving into something difficult is that, every day, you know a little more. The more you know, the easier it gets.

Every time I do a speech, I search for current trends and challenges for the industry the audience works in. "What are trends in the medical device and equipment industry?" There are always many, many sites that list what is going on.

Let go of your fear and decide to learn one thing.

Remember my on-ramp to the information superhighway. It's not all that hard. Dive in.

7

Those Millennials

"Who the hell do they think they are? Entitled! They don't play by the rules! They haven't worked long enough or hard enough to march into the CEO's office like that. They, they, they . . . they don't know their place!"

Oh yeah, the millennials caused quite a commotion when they showed up at work.

There was a very loud "tsk-tsk" from the boomers.

That hysterical, judgmental snub from so many baby boomers and Gen Xers was a mistake that has backfired badly. The millennials were smart. They've done well. Now they are taking charge.

Millennials, born between 1981 and 1996, grew up with technology and can do more with their thumbs than most of us can do with our whole bodies. They may not act the way you want them to act, but they sure have earned their place and they have plenty to teach us—and, absolutely, much to learn from us as well.

If we are ever going to work with them, we need to understand them.

Gallup estimates we have seventy-three million millennials in the workplace. Their influence grows as ten thousand baby boomers (born between 1946 and 1964) leave the workforce to retire every day. They make up more than half of the workforce now, and in five years it'll be 75 percent.

Millennials want their work to be recognized for their actual contribution, and if they are killing it on day one, they want to be rewarded and respected accordingly. They don't expect or want their job to last forever, whether they pack up and go or get fired or laid off. For them, every job and assignment is an opportunity to increase their skills and boost their power to contribute elsewhere.

The hiring process often is completely different from how it used to be. Instead of deciding whether the applicant can meet expectations and satisfy demands, recruiters find themselves selling their companies to applicants, focusing on what these sought-after applicants are looking for and what the companies can give them. They focus on what these bright applicants are seeking in their careers as well as what they want for their home lives.

I know what some of you are thinking. The hiring managers for every job you ever applied for wanted to know what *you* could do for *them*.

Instead of labeling the younger generation as demanding, privileged, or whiny, it is in your interest to reach out and connect.

Reach Out to *Them*

"You're not right because you are older," explained millennial Zach Friedman, an innovator who works for Nationwide. "You are not more knowledgeable because you have had more years in the workplace. Don't speak down to us. Millennials may have less of your experience, but may have more experience in things you are not experienced in. We're all just trying to figure it out. We are all just people."

One of my mentors, Kyla Thompson, laid it out this way: it's time to get rid of the anger at millennials and stop joking about them or getting irritated.

"That is something that will never work," said Thompson, a groundbreaking crisis-management expert who impressed me years ago when she was killing it in Denver.

"Part of aging is having to work with younger generations. Don't make fun of millennials. They are here. They aren't going away. They are wonderfully talented. Learn how to work with them, rather than resist them. Young people don't want to be told what to do, but they do want to be inspired by you."

Working with millennials means showing you are not judging them or lording your experience over them. You have to show them you are willing to go on a journey with them to be a true colleague or partner.

To work with them, we need to understand who they are. I practically got a college degree in millennialism from Amy Shea, a branded communications consultant and strategist who, as a baby boomer, sought work late in her career and, because of her profession, knows generational data and the realities.

Shea learned plenty from her daughter and her friends to get feedback on this subject, something I suggest every person with access to younger people do. Talk, talk, talk with younger people.

Shea is popular with her daughter's friends because she doesn't lecture or give advice. She will sometimes tell stories about her life. "She said, 'I'm not teaching, I'm not an older person talking down to them, I'm not explaining things to them. I'm just sharing.'"

She's seen many people her age do those things to younger people, and it backfired. "They'd say, 'Don't worry about that. When I was in my twenties, that stuff happens.' There was a desire to go down memory lane and explain life to them. I found that dismissive to the idea that *they* have something to teach *me* about how the world works now."

There can be a natural bridge between the baby boomer generation and the millennials because both generations were mission driven and believed they could turn the world around, she said. Boomers had their callings: civil rights, peace, the environment. Those things led to mass social protest movements in the 1960s. Millennials have that same passion but feel personally responsible for turning the world around; they do it differently, powerfully, often by working in small groups of people who share their missions. They have powerful social consciousness and, if a brand misbehaves, the millennials will defect.

"The attitude millennials have is they are empowered to create the life they want to create. What describes baby boomers better than that? Who went off the grid? 'No, thanks, I'm not going to go to Vietnam. No, thanks, I am not going to sit on the back of the bus. No, thanks, I'm not going to be paid less than you.'"

"There are so many assumptions about who millennials are and what they want, and they are making assumptions about who we are and what we want," she said. "We are the most linked two generations that have existed in history." And remember, Shea's own research looks at the statistical profiles of how human beings react and behave.

When Shea started her job, she realized it worked in her favor that she is an avant-garde dresser. She looked cool. Younger people came to see her as a resource with whom, as colleagues, they could joke.

She said there is nothing a millennial hates more than doing something the way it's always been done when there is a smarter way to proceed. "They want a give-and-take and they are very accustomed to it. They move at great speeds. They were raised on technology. Nothing makes them crazier than making them do something when they know a computer could do it."

Focus on a communication bridge.

"We bring up our age, we bring up how things were back in the day. We send the signal to the millennial that we think we are different from them. It's not better, it's not worse. But, as soon as you set up a difference, you are making a mistake. Don't make differences that should not exist," she said.

She's the oldest person in her office, but she decided at the beginning that she was going to learn from her younger colleagues. She sought *their* point of view, rather than pontificating her own. "I work *with* them."

Don't create divides when you don't have to.

"If you want to stay current, you have to accept that this is a world connected by technology," she said. Communicate the way they communicate. Use the technology they use. Don't create differences.

Don't Talk Down to Them

Millennial Jimmy Madden laid it out for me.

"Communication through technology is the biggest thing," said Madden, a cybersecurity specialist who is a millennial. "If the older generation isn't keeping up with technology because they are choosing to be stubborn, then they'll be behind because the way to communicate is through social media or texting. Phone calls and emails are things younger people don't want to bother with."

If his phone rings, it's a bother.

"Text me and you'll get an answer. Don't call me because I am not going to answer," he said. "You can access email through your phone, but younger people don't like email because it is loaded with junk. We aren't associating it with communication."

It's irritating when they are criticized for being on their phones all the time. "Yeah, we are on our phones, but that is taking the place of a computer, books, magazines, newspapers, TV, news channels, and everything else that is on our phone that we used to deal with elsewhere. We are constantly taking in new information and learning. We are consuming massive amounts of information," he said.

"A big turnoff for a younger person is when someone who is old enough to be their parent talks to them as if they are not as smart, responsible, educated, or experienced," he said. A twenty-year-old has consumed massive amounts of information already—waaaaay more than a twenty-year-old consumed thirty years ago.

"My nephew is six, but he was only two when he was teaching me how to use a new Nintendo game console and telling me all about it," Madden said. "That right there should tell you something. By the time my nephew is six, he will have been using things that many older people haven't even tried."

The Anatomy of a Millennial

Todd Cherches has studied millennials in the workplace on a number of levels. He is one part academic, one part leadership expert, and one part consultant. He teaches at both New York University and Columbia University in their schools of professional studies. He's widely quoted as an expert on millennials—even though he is a baby boomer.

He chuckles because boomers so often gripe about millennials being entitled or having attitudes.

"Well, who were they raised by? The baby boomers! It's hard to generalize a whole generation, but millennials are motivated by three things: freedom, money, and purpose. Baby boomers were okay paying their dues for years and saying, 'I'll get there eventually.' Millennials want it from day one, and if they don't get it, they will leave."

They are willing to work hard, but they don't want to do things that are menial or trivial. They don't want to waste time and are impatient. They want feedback *now,* he said. Millennials want to start a job that is meaningful and stimulating where they will get constant feedback, but that is a key pet peeve of baby boomer bosses because they feel millennials always want a pat on the back.

Millennials are too casual and informal for baby boomers. That's how they were raised, so they have no problem knocking on the door of the CEO's office with a complaint or an idea, Cherches said. They'll send the CEO an email, when we would never have done that. To them, there is no hierarchy.

The millennial wants to be treated as a person, not a position. Baby boomers often had bosses who didn't even know their names.

Millennials do take work seriously, he said, but only if they believe what they are doing matters. They will not do busywork or menial work for long. They want to know that it matches their skills. They want to be mentally stimulated. Social impact is very important to millennials. It's not just a paycheck to them.

And if a millennial is your boss?

"Leave your ego at the door," Cherches said. "Phrases like, 'When I was your age . . .' or, "When I first started . . ." are not good. Show respect for them and show that you value their opinion. Don't act like you are their parent. You are not their father or mother. Respect their title. Still, they do look to you for your experience in the world. There is a fine line. You don't want to say, 'Back in 1995 . . .' but you can communicate that you once dealt with a similar situation and here's what happened. It's not about showing how smart you are, it's about showing what you can contribute."

What you wear matters. If you are used to wearing a suit and tie and the people around you are wearing jeans, wear jeans or khakis. Otherwise, they assume you don't fit into their culture, he said.

The key thing is adding value and understanding the business and the language they use, Cherches said. Use metaphors and analogies they relate to. Always be respectful.

Give Them a Chance

"One of the things I like the most about millennials or younger people, which I think sometimes aggravates people in the workforce, is they don't want to wait until they're promoted to a certain position to have influence," said Shelley Broader, former CEO of Chicos FAS and a former regional CEO of Walmart. "They don't understand why a good idea can't be executed right away."

Her daughter doesn't want to wait her turn to be heard and have influence. Broader has come to wonder why the status quo doesn't want to listen.

"Really, why can't a good idea be executed right away?" she asks. "And the truth is, she won't wait to have her turn. She will find a place where she can have influence."

She can operate that way because she doesn't have to chase the same reward and motivation system that Broader and other baby boomers did.

"Baby boomers were taught to give up freedom and happiness for money and power," Broader said. "If you want to be really powerful and make a lot of money, you have to go through a lot of sacrifices and give up a lot of personal freedoms because it is your duty to have all this money and power. But the younger generation will gladly give up money and power to have happiness, freedom, and influence. There are people who think, 'Aren't they stupid?' But I think, 'Aren't they brilliant?'"

I received valuable perspective on how to work with millennials from Sara Treaster, age thirty-two.

"Start from a place of trust. Your younger colleagues might not have as much experience, but that doesn't mean they don't know what they are doing and it doesn't mean that they haven't worked very hard to get where they are."

If they don't do it your way, but they still get it done—or get it done better—what's the crime?

My algebra teacher used to hate the shortcuts I created to solve problems. I always got the right answer, but I didn't follow the rules to get to it. What difference did it make?

"From my point of view, titles and the hierarchical trappings are just sort of red tape in the way," Treaster said. "They don't really matter. What matters is getting the job done, hopefully having a good time while you are doing it, and connecting on a person-to-person level."

Life balance is nonnegotiable with younger workers. It's mandatory. But don't assume they are not committed because they aren't working around the clock.

"My generation has incredibly hard workers because we came of age during the recession and we had to fight for everything we have," she said. "But we realize that work isn't everything. I work so I can live my life. I don't live my life to work."

The best way to communicate is to dive into what will make everyone more successful: cross-mentoring. Younger people want to learn; they just don't like being talked down to.

"It works really well when both parties approach each other

from a place of respect, rather than 'You don't know that, how dumb you are . . .'" Treaster said.

Be open and patient because it takes patience on both sides. Millennials have a valuable mental agility that we should learn from. Those young people aren't the enemy. They are becoming our leaders. Yes, they are very, very different, but it's time to open up to all they have to offer.

8

Coming Back at Work

I have a friend who was in a foul mood the day of her annual evaluation. When her boss highlighted three areas where she met rather than exceeded expectations, she stood up, looked at her boss, and said, "Well, if that's the way you feel, I quit." So she did.

Fortunately she was in her twenties, unbelievably talented, and soon was hired somewhere else.

I worked with another reporter who grabbed her purse, told the city desk she was heading out for lunch, then never came back. The incredible part of that story is that she (a) got a much better job very quickly and (b) was hired back years later to the very paper she'd walked out of!

Oh, to have those options! Things would be so much easier. But most of us don't have those options, and before you bolt out the door, I want to make sure we spend some time looking at how you might be able to orchestrate a comeback right where you are. I support your packing up your talent and leaving. But if that is your route, take time to make sure you are positioned for a speedy, successful change. You should have your network, résumé, cover letter, and plan ready before you decide it is time to go because doing so makes it much easier for you to quickly land a new job.

So how can you stage a comeback right where you are?

Is Your Job Salvageable?

Don't make the decision to bolt because you are bored or angry. You don't know if the next place might be just as difficult as where you are. Look around you, size up who you are working for, and try to figure out the likelihood that your boss or situation will improve. If not, talk to people in other companies to see if the things that are annoying you are happening in their companies as well. If not, start looking. If so, start looking for ways to make peace with where you are currently employed.

Take a time-out to stop fixating on what your company is doing wrong.

Make a list of twenty things that you like about your company.

Now make a list of twenty things you have learned while you have been there.

Finally, make a list of twenty reasons why other people would want your job.

If you truly are trying to be positive and can't come up with those lists, just skip to the part where it's time to pack up your talent and go.

I have a coaching client who wanted to leave her Fortune 200 company pronto because she hated the culture change, didn't like the people in charge, and was oh so ready to move on.

But after she made her list of what she learned there, she started to appreciate everything the company had allowed her to learn and accomplish. She'd enjoyed opportunities that paid off in promotions, huge responsibilities, and an enormous salary. That company grew her up.

She still wants to make a change, but going into gratitude instead of toxic reaction mode was the antidote that bought her the peace of mind to slow down and come up with the right plan for her and her family. More than a year later, she's still there. She's still planning to make a change, but she's not being reactive.

So is there any way to pull back, slow down, and get a little more comfortable where you are so you can make the decision that is right for you?

Develop Yourself So You Become More Valuable

If things are a little sluggish for you at work, let's get you back on the radar as a viable, go-to player. When that works, will your morale improve?

If you are waiting for your company to train you on new technology and prepare you for coming trends, you are branding yourself irrelevant. It is on you to develop yourself, and it is so easy to do it. Follow the instructions in this book on staying up on trends in your industry and the right publications to learn the latest. Always add new skills to your repertoire. It is so easy to continue your education with online classes that are either free or inexpensive.

Make your growth clear to your peers and bosses by talking about new learning that may be relevant to what the company is doing. Pass along articles you have read. This lifts your profile as an active learner *and* shows you are someone who will help the company move into the future.

Look at what the favored employees are doing in technology. How are they using social media? Are you keeping up?

It is a *huge* mistake for you to do things the way you have always done them with the skills that have always helped you deliver. It is so important to constantly add new skills and update yourself. Technology is changing so fast and making it easy for companies to eliminate so many people in the workforce. Your refusal to update and upskill yourself will brand you as irrelevant and make you vulnerable to cuts—even if you are doing good work.

Make sure you read the chapter "How to Catch Up" and start acting on it today.

Be First to Dive into Change

Change is constant. If you can't accept it and be an early adapter, just take a Sharpie and write the word HACK on your forehead, because you will be in the way and largely ineffective.

Managers have always hated dealing with employees who whine about change. Change just *is*. It is a constant, it is inevitable, and you either make it easy on your company or hard. Who is going to be rewarded?

There have been many studies on change. Yes, some people adapt to it easier than others, but you can train yourself to be more adaptive.

1. Accept that change is coming and there is no way to avoid it.
2. Decide to dive into it so you will be the first to benefit from mastering it.
3. Realize that the more you do this, the easier it gets.

Always try to be prepared so you know what is coming, and do your advance work to educate yourself on how that will change your job, your department, and the whole company. Be the first to be trained and make it clear you wish to help others dealing with the changes. If you publicly and positively embrace the changes, you will acquire a reputation as someone helping drive the company's future. If you resist, you are at best an annoyance and at worst a problem. You will make yourself vulnerable and expendable. It doesn't matter if you liked things better the old way or even if the old way seemed to work better. The faster you accept, cope, and adapt, the faster you become a go-to change leader.

Even if you hate the new changes or if they aren't working, keep your mouth shut. Things will continue to change. Just accept it and work with what you've got.

Use Meetings to Showcase Yourself

Used properly, a staff or committee meeting is the perfect opportunity to advertise who you are and what you are delivering to your company. That said, many people are meeting flops because they don't prepare in advance and come with no strategy of what they wish to accomplish. So here is my strategy for being noticed and heard in a meeting:

1. Prepare.
2. Study the agenda.
3. Pick your topic, or get on the agenda and present something.
4. Know what you want to say. One idea, three bullet points.
5. Get advance support and return the favor.
6. Arrive early.
7. Work the room.
8. Speak first.
9. Be clear and concise.
10. No wimpy language like "I think . . . ," "I feel . . . ," "In my opinion . . . ," or "This might be a dumb idea, but . . ."

Share your perspective, but be very, very careful about polluting it with reminders that you've been there, done that, and that you know best because you are sooo experienced. Get rid of the "If it ain't broke, don't fix it" mentality. Otherwise, you are the curmudgeon dragging everybody down, lost in the past and unwilling to embrace the future.

Make Your Coworkers Love You Even More

It is hard to dump a revered member of the team. Make sure you regularly compliment your coworkers on their work, their pictures of their kids, their new hairstyle, whatever. Just be the nicest person in the whole office.

That does not protect you, but I have seen some pretty incompetent coworkers keep their jobs many years after they should have been fired, simply because they were so well liked. Companies do fire people who are beloved, but managers think twice about it. Plus, it is not that hard to be kind to others.

On the flip side, managers have no problem dumping on or getting rid of the employees who are high maintenance or not well liked. They almost get cheered for it. If you've assumed that all you had to do is come to work and deliver, you missed a great opportunity to make yourself valuable by doing the easiest thing of all: being nice.

If that is hard for you, well, I have to introduce you to Carolyn Little, one of the most popular people in any workplace because she was so good to be around. I once told her that she should train me on tact and diplomacy, and she admitted, "I just manipulate people with kindness."

Huh?

She says you can't lose by being kind. It has to be genuine, because if it isn't, people will sense that and it will backfire. But she has three possible scenarios where kindness will help you to get exactly what you want:

1. *Being nice to somebody who is being mean to you.* "You steal all the thunder out of their meanness and you steal all the satisfaction they get from being mean to you."
2. *Being nice to somebody who is indifferent.* "They'll be nicer to you—probably without even realizing it."
3. *Being nice to somebody who is already nice.* "That's the easy one."

Is it any wonder why she is always beloved?

Step Up

Volunteer like crazy. If there is a committee, get on it. If you see an unmet need, draft a proposal to solve it, then submit it, stepping up to do or oversee the work yourself. Make yourself a player by being a player.

It is amazing how you can expand your authority and reach by taking on new assignments without demanding a raise or a title. As you grow your reach, you can then position yourself to get the title and the raise. But first start delivering more at a higher level than you are currently delivering.

Write down a list of things you could do to make the company more successful. Then pick one and strategize how you would carry out your plan. Once you know what you can do and how you would do it, find the right opportunity to make your presentation. Bosses love people who are willing to take on extra responsibilities without creating more work for them.

As you do these extra assignments, keep everybody in the

loop with emails or texts. This keeps you on their radar as someone who is actively making a difference.

Stop Listening to Other People's Gripes

Want to hate your job? Just start listening to the others in the
office who hate theirs. While you need to hear the gossip about what
the company may or may not be doing, keep your mouth shut, repeat nothing, and walk away when people start complaining.

When you listen to the bitching, you start to feel horrible
about this little thing or that. It feeds on itself and festers. You
add your angst to the next person's and the next, and suddenly
it seems as if you are working in the worst place on earth when
you probably aren't.

A very successful salesperson recently told me she wants to
get out of her company because her employer is now charging
her $3,000 a year toward her insurance premiums, and she was
used to paying nothing. Nobody wants to suddenly have to pay
that kind of money, but all I could think of was how much my
premiums have increased. I'm paying nearly $12,000 a year—
just for premiums—and there have been huge increases every
year. She sees this as a $3,000 reduction in salary. And, while
some employers are kicking in more toward insurance coverage
than hers, most are contributing substantially less.

So my question to her was, Are you going to go into a loop,
fixate on that $3,000, get all mad, decide to leave, then look for
another job where you might have to pay the same amount of
money or even more?

She's got a good job. Not perfect, but she likes it. The more
she and the others around her complain about that health insurance premium, the more it seems like a big problem. But there
are so many dozens of news stories in the last three years with

headlines like, "Employees' Share of Health Costs Continues Rising Faster Than Wages." Never mind everyone who has been laid off with no health benefits.

Just stop focusing on what you hate, look at what you love, and then decide if it can work.

Change Your Mindset

Jobs are like marriages. Good days, bad days, and you either continue to commit or you walk away. There is always something to complain about with your job, but don't fall into that trap.

Instead, refocus so you can start feeling as good about your job as you felt the day you got the offer.

1. Chill. Be mindful, be calm, purposefully say positive things to remind yourself of all the good things you get in your current situation.

2. Don't obsess over your boss. One way or another, that situation is going to change. Either your boss moves up or out, or you do. Your boss does not own you forever. He or she is only a temporary player in your life who has a little say over your life—temporarily.

3. Assign yourself stress-free moments, either by taking short breaks or waiting to meditate when you get home. Practice mindfulness so you are not stressed.

4. Read Dale Carnegie's *How to Win Friends and Influence People*. This classic was written in 1936 and is one of the bestselling books of all time—for a reason. It shows you how to be effective with people. The advice is timeless and will make you happier with your current situation—and more successful.

5. Don't try to win every battle. Sometimes you will see your bosses making big mistakes. I remember

newspaper editor Rosemary O'Hara telling me to learn when to let things go. "It's like you are bowling and you see a ball that is destined to be a gutter ball. Sometimes you have to wave at the ball as it rolls toward the gutter and just say, 'Bye-bye.' Let it go." Even if you think you know better, you don't always have to say it.

Dealing with a Bosshole

There are some people that even Dale Carnegie couldn't cure. I worked for one of them. You probably have, too. I call these jerks in management "bossholes." I did not invent the word, but I sure do love it.

We got a new boss at the newspaper where I worked. He was an absolute bully, yelling at his people and driving out a number of exceedingly talented employees because, apparently, he couldn't stand anyone smarter, stronger, or more talented than he was. My professional goal was to become a columnist, and one day he called me into his office and said, "You think you're going to be a columnist? You will never be a columnist. All you are now is all you will ever be. A reporter."

Well, I proved him wrong.

But all he was then was all he would ever be: A flaming bosshole.

Everybody connects with that story when I tell it because everybody has had a bad boss. But I owe that jerk a lot because, had he not been such a bully, I'd have stayed in that job until that newspaper went out of business, which it did after I left. If I'd stayed, I would have been struggling to find my way in the world in a profession that was quickly dying.

There are bad bosses you can win over and bad bosses you can't.

What triggers your bosshole? Is he or she angry because you take a long lunch or come in late? Don't take a long lunch or come in late. If it is missed deadlines, don't miss your deadline.

If you are being made miserable by a micromanager, get into that person's head and figure out what that person is going to want from you before it is ever requested. That way, when you are asked for something, you can say, "Here it is . . ." The better you are at anticipating what the person wants, the less he or she will tell you what to do.

Career coach and writer Dorianne St Fleur wrote a blog article revealing three statements that help de-escalate things when your boss is coming at you:

1. "I'm sorry I [insert mistake]."
2. "I understand why this happened."
3. "What I've learned from my mistake is [insert what you've learned]."

I love those three simple statements because they can help you tame the beast. When I was a kid and I messed up, I found the best way to stop my mom from endlessly lecturing me was to say, "You're right." And she'd lecture a little bit more and I'd say, "Mom, I already told you that you are right." After that, the lecture would stop and I would be living in peace again.

Many people become unnerved because their boss stops communicating with them altogether, which is, of course, a bad sign. If meetings get canceled or conversations are clipped, something is up. When that happens, don't stop trying—take action.

Schedule an appointment and be ready to share accomplishments and what you are working on. Ask for feedback on what you should prioritize. Then, start sending weekly emails summarizing what you are working on. This documents your work and shows you are making an effort to communicate.

Also, make sure your bosshole is really a bosshole. When under attack, it is very easy to make assumptions about your boss.

Back when I was an editor, I had an employee who thought I was a horrible boss. He liked being an investigative reporter who would do a story every month or so, but my bosses hired me to clean shop. They thought he was lazy and unproductive. The day I started my job there, they told me they wanted him out. He'd been there a long time and had done some good work, and I asked that they let me work with him on productivity. The managing editor told me that the only way he could stay was to write a story every single day, no matter what. The reporter assumed I was mean and riding him hard. He had no idea that I was fighting to keep him employed.

He finally quit, furious with me. He never realized that I was the one who kept him from being fired months earlier.

So, if you are angry with your boss, make sure the anger isn't misplaced.

Also, don't make too many assumptions about the person who is making you miserable. I once worked for a woman everybody hated. She was always sucking up to the big boss while dumping her stupid ideas on the rest of us. Years later, she told me she knew she was hated, but she was actually terrified in her job because she worried she wasn't ready for it and was always scared she would get fired.

We just thought she was a brownnosing jerk.

So don't make assumptions. Dig a little deeper.

Is this person a jerk to everybody, or just you?

Is this person really coming after you?

Does this person just want different performance?

Is it possible this person is trying to help you do better work?

Warning Signs

Sometimes you get the feeling that something is wrong and that your job may be in jeopardy.

Aside from external factors like budget cuts or a corporate sale or merger, there are internal factors that suggest you may be right. For example:

- You are being excluded from meetings.
- You aren't getting the raises or promotions you expect and deserve.
- Your work is being scrutinized.
- You are being criticized or mocked. (Address this. Have an honest discussion about the criticism. Is it true? How can you improve? If it's not true, make your case without sounding overly prickly or defensive.)
- The good assignments are all going to other people.
- You are being micromanaged worse than ever. (This can be a sign that they are starting to document a case against you, but you can document in reverse with emails giving updates, passing on compliments from others, and repeating verbal compliments your boss may have given you.)
- You feel you are being kept in the dark about changes or other happenings in the office. (Ask for updates on the specific issues you aren't being told about.)
- Your projects are being assigned to others.

If it seems obvious that something is up, set a meeting with your boss. Let him or her know how important your job is to you and that you want to do whatever it takes to make you a key player there. Say, "If I need to make changes, I will make them.

I am committed to this job and want to deliver everything you expect from me—and more." Then prove it.

It is hard to turn an opinion around, but it can definitely be done. After that major clash with my bosshole, when he condemned me to being a reporter for the rest of my life, a surprise dream opportunity was handed to me from the news corporation that owned our newspaper. The guy in charge of all nationally syndicated columns wanted me to write one. As I mentioned, that was my lifelong dream.

But, as quickly as my excitement soared, my bosshole intervened. He was furious the corporate guy had done and end run around him without consulting him and demanded the offer be retracted. I worked for him, and he wasn't having it.

That was too much for me.

I slacked off. I came in late, left early. At some point, I realized I was angering my coworkers and my direct boss, not just the bosshole. But I thought about it, and honestly I wasn't doing my best. I was trying to punish him by giving less of myself, but that let everybody else down. I met my city editor in the cafeteria and said, "I know I have been slacking off, and I know you are upset. I am done with that now." I started generating major stories that won numerous awards. Without my even applying, she promoted me into an editing position, and I felt I'd made my comeback. But, surprise, the bosshole heard the news, and he stepped in and killed my promotion. I learned a lot that year. You punish yourself when you let a bad boss's behavior affect your performance. And I learned there is no hope for some bossholes.

Which led to my final takeaway from that experience: you can always pack up your talent and go.

That is what I finally did. It wouldn't matter if I'd won a

Pulitzer Prize. That bad boss was intent on derailing my career. By leaving, I found a bigger paycheck and a better job and moved to warm Florida, near my family. It also was the step that led to my second career as an author and speaker.

My greatest success was born out of what felt at the time like my greatest failure.

Be Ready to Move On

The idea of having to look for work inspires fear that can be avoided if you just do what you need to do to be ready. Some people dread writing their résumé so much that they stay in jobs they hate for years. Never mind that they can easily hire someone else to write it for them, or they can do it themselves in a day.

If you are going to have confidence, make yourself ready for anything. That way, you can choose to leave your company—or not. Or if you get the boot and are fired or laid off, all you have to do is hit the switch on your magnificently organized plan so you can get hired quickly.

Check out "Letter to Dave," the next chapter. Dave is frozen in that deer-in-the-headlights moment, where he knows change is coming and hasn't done anything to insulate himself. Also, read the chapters on getting hired.

Then spend the next month diving into all the things you are dreading. If you set deadlines for yourself ("I'll get my résumé done no later than 7:00 p.m. Sunday"), you can power through the tasks rather quickly. "Letter to Dave" is your guide.

Your confidence will increase because you aren't in victim mode, waiting for someone else to tell you what you need to do and when you need to do it. You will be in action mode, by choice, and you will be taking control of what had previously felt like a chaotic experience.

You should always be prepared to move on because the

workplace is so unpredictable. Management is constantly changing. Companies are coming, going, buying, selling. Veteran employees are being dumped for money-saving machines that can do the same work. If you already have an idea of where you would like to go and have planted the right seeds in your network, you will be so much better off than if you show up for work one day, are called into HR and told, "We'll be terminating your position immediately," or "We've restructured and yours is one of the positions we will be eliminating." That is going to hurt like hell, no matter what. But it is going to hurt a whole lot less if you have already thought through the what-ifs and have a plan for the steps you will take next.

So if you aren't ready to go, get ready to go. It doesn't mean you have to go, it just means you are insuring yourself against uncertainty. You are controlling the things you can control. If you haven't done the steps in the "Letter to Dave," do them this week. Next week at the latest.

Then watch your stress level go down.

9

Letter to Dave

I wrote this letter to my friend's husband when he was concerned his job was going to be cut in a merger. It's a crash course on what to do when you need to save your career quickly.

Hi, Dave . . .

I heard your company is going to be acquired and your job might be eliminated in the next few weeks. Here is my advice on how to quickly confront the situation and find new employment.

First, remember your greatest opportunity to get a new job is within the first five weeks of losing your old one. So the time to get things moving is right now, before you are out of work, so you can immediately hit the switch when it is time. The way to avoid worry paralysis is to take action.

What to do:

1. **Start a to-do list** and give yourself tight deadlines for everything on it. Devote at least one hour every day to this list before the acquisition. This will help you get perfectly positioned and reduce your stress level.

2. **Pick ten companies** you'd most like to work for. Study them. Find people who you can connect to on LinkedIn so you have at least five contacts within the company. Send these strangers requests and say you are interested in their company and you wonder if you might ask them a few questions. Start cultivating those resources, because the minute an opening becomes available, you can start to leverage the connection. Or if you stay on their radar, they can tell you about opportunities you won't know about.

3. **Get your résumé ready.** You'll need multiple versions because a customized résumé is much more successful than a one-size-fits-all you send to everybody. Keep it to one page. You've been with your company for seventeen years. The trick is to not show potential employers that you are over fifty. So wipe the dates and list titles and the company. List skills. (See my chapter on getting hired.)

4. **Pump up your LinkedIn profile.** This is critical. There are many good videos on how to use LinkedIn. Start watching them because LinkedIn can make your life so much easier. Start posting three times a week to show your interest and expertise in your subject. Keep expanding your network. People get unsolicited job inquiries all the time because of their LinkedIn profiles.

5. **Sign up for workitdaily.com,** which gives you affordable advice and personal coaching from a real expert.

6. **Figure out what's ahead in your industry.** Start studying trends in your industry so you have something to talk about with people in your network and

during job interviews. Search online for "trends in _____ industry" and you'll get up to speed. Then start posting that stuff on LinkedIn with a few paragraphs of your opinion or analysis. All of this helps position you as someone who is current.

7. **Pick five people** to add to your network, then write quick emails for informational interviews. If you already know them, just ask them if you can pick their brains. If they are people you are trying to add into your network, write a good note that says, "Can I buy you a cup of coffee to get your thoughts on what is happening in the industry and what it is like at (name of company)? My current company is going to be acquired and your input would be a real help." Have a list of questions ready and don't monopolize the person's time. Do try to find some personal connection so you can work to turn this person into a more valuable contact who will actually make calls for you. (Read the networking chapter.) Follow up with a thank-you note.

8. **Put the word out there.** Start telling people in your professional network *and* your friend network that you are making a change and need any suggestions and help they can give you.

9. **Start going to meetings of professional groups** in your industry. Make friends, not just business contacts. These people will know what jobs are out there and lead you to them before anything is even posted.

10. **Become familiar with job websites** and the jobs they are posting. Remember, at your age, your best entrée is through someone who works at the company, which is why your networking strategy is most important.

11. **Take online classes.** You may be very skilled in what you need to do your job today, but it is time to learn what you need to be proficient in over the next five years. Do that by checking out edx.org and coursera .org and take some FREE online classes offered by premier universities around the world. These will make you more interesting and viable. This "upskilling" helps justify your current salary level.

And a few don'ts:

1. **Don't take a time-out.** Especially if you want to maintain your status and salary, you have to be ready to roll. Even if you deserve a fabulous vacation, resist the temptation. The longer you wait, the harder it gets. Take the vacation after your initial five to six weeks of job hunting.

2. **Don't assume this is the beginning of your career's decline** or a slow slide into retirement. You've got another decade (or more) in front of you. You can fall in love with a whole new challenge and make more money and be fabulously happy.

3. **Don't give up on your current company.** They are going to keep *some* people, and you might make the cut if you show ideas that will help as the company embraces the latest technology. Do *not* position yourself as the best person for the job today. Position yourself as the best person for the job five years from today.

10

Branding Your Relevance

Bobbie's This 'n' That opened up in a tiny strip mall in my little town a few years back. The location and the exterior presented challenges: the building was separated from all the activity on the main street through town, and the store's only windows were six feet off the ground, stripped across the top of the storefront to let light in. The storefront was blocked by a wall of bricks.

There was no way to know what was going on in there. What were they selling? Was anyone even there?

Since it took an effort, I never stopped in to check. There were never any cars in front of the store. Many of us wondered why it had such a vague name if you couldn't see inside or figure out what on earth Bobbie was selling.

One day, it went out of business.

A few months later, I needed a watch battery and stopped at the jewelry store that was located next to where Bobbie's had been located.

"Hey, what did they sell in that store next door?" I asked the salesclerk.

"Purses, accessories—you know, just this and that," said the woman.

"I always wondered why the store had that name, This 'n' That. What a stupid name for a business. It didn't tell me anything about what was in the store, and you couldn't see inside," I said.

"I'm Bobbie," said the woman.

Gulp.

Honestly, so many people run their careers like Bobbie's This 'n' That. They hide what they are offering and they wonder why they aren't getting any notice. They don't take the time to brand themselves or even figure out what their brand is.

If you haven't defined your personal brand, you are leaving it to others to define it for you. Few will make the effort. Few people ever stopped by Bobbie's This 'n' That to see what was for sale. But if her business name had let me know what she was selling or if she'd installed a window showcasing what was inside, she might still be in business.

Do people know what it is that separates you from everybody else?

Do you?

Because if you can't articulate that, nobody is going to know what separates you from the pack—unless they make the effort to figure it out.

Your brand should show you are relevant, viable, and a player in your industry.

Grab a cup of coffee, because you are about to get a million-dollar coaching session with the number-one expert on personal branding, William Arruda. Arruda is a bestselling author, as well as a go-to trainer and keynote speaker for the world's largest corporations. He is a regular columnist for Forbes.

Personal branding is his brand.

"If you can't immediately demonstrate relevance at work, you will be discounted," Arruda said. "There are a lot of people out there who feel like reluctant relics. They're stuck. What they really need to become is relevant change agents."

And if you are searching for work, your personal brand is even more important.

If your personal brand is "irrelevance," you have a problem. Who is going to bet on someone who is known for being dated or a has-been?

Perception is reality. Even if the perception of you is undeserved or wrong, it is a key measure of whether you will be hired or how you will be valued and advanced. It is on you to build a brand that makes you indispensable.

If you want job security, brand yourself as relevant, viable, and the face of the future. Advertise what you contribute and what you will offer in five and ten years.

What is it, exactly, that you offer that no one else does? What is your "special sauce"?

When you market yourself as the expert and the go-to person in a unique and vital category, you raise your visibility. It shows why you are taking up oxygen in the office and justifies your share of the payroll budget.

Over time, the need to self-market increases. It doesn't decrease as it did in the past when employees were respected and rewarded based on their years of loyal service. Now, you must advertise what it is that you offer. If you don't do this, you are always at risk of falling into the chasm of marginally necessary or mostly useless employees. If you are in the hiring pool, defining your brand is especially important so you get noticed as someone who is a player deserving of consideration.

Your Special Sauce

First, figure out what differentiates you. If you don't have something, *get it*. There are limitless opportunities to learn more and grow your worth. As you start to study your industry and trends, you can incorporate the future into your branding. Don't position yourself for where you are but where you want to be down the road.

"Look at the skills you have and the expertise you bring to the table, and see how that is relevant," Arruda said. "When you have answered those questions, ask yourself why people come to you. When people introduce you, what words do they use to describe you? What would other people say are your greatest strengths? If you start thinking about that and interview people you have worked with, you can start to get clear about what stands out and makes you compelling. You need a today, tomorrow, and end-of-career strategy."

If you visualize what you want to have accomplished at the end of your career, it helps you create a path that otherwise is uncertain because of the rate of change in the workplace. You might not be able to choose the title and job you want in five or ten years because it may no longer exist. But you can have an idea of the path that will make you fulfilled.

This is all the more important as companies change the whole paradigm of staffing.

"The job market is moving from an active one to a passive one, where people will find you, rather than the other way around. You won't have to actively pursue opportunity, which is great, but if you are not crystal clear about who you are, what your value is, and why people should care, people are not going to find you and bring you in to do their projects."

The Right LinkedIn Profile Will Beat a Résumé

"Competition has increased tremendously because we can hire the best no matter where they are located," Arruda said. "More and more work is being done remotely, so you now compete with, potentially, millions of people across the world. How do you make yourself so desirable that people are willing to pay more for you? There are a million people who can do what every one of us does. You need to offer something that is in addition, something valuable to the people making the decisions. So, first of all, you need to figure out what that differentiation is, what makes you stand out, what is that unique secret sauce that you deliver that is going to be relevant and compelling to the people making decisions about you, so people will choose you over others, even if you are more expensive. What gives you the value that makes it worth it?"

Have you thought about this? Many people have not. They get on a career track and let the job—not their individual assets and talents—define them. Is it better to be known as the "HR person" or the person who is the best negotiator or the best at dealing with problem employees or the best at recruiting minorities or the best at training new leaders or the best at using technology for recruiting? Don't define your brand with your job. Define it with your strengths.

This is increasingly important as more jobs are eliminated by technology. What can you do if artificial intelligence or robotics is wiping out your specialty? Arruda says you shouldn't freak yourself out about it.

"I don't know why everyone focuses on the negative side of jobs disappearing," he said. "They panic that, 'Oh my God, the jobs we have today are not going to be here tomorrow!' Well, the good news is the new jobs that *will* be here tomorrow, I think they are going to be far more exciting and far more interesting. We don't know what they are yet, but a lot of the things we hate about our jobs, how tedious they are, those are the things that will go away. And the things that will be needed will be much more high-level and strategic, which requires a human brain and heart to make happen."

You need to know more in order to take advantage of those new opportunities. If you are not learning every day, you are barreling toward insignificance. Don't wait for your boss to tell you it is time to take a training course. You have to be on top of it. You decide the skills you want and need based on what you are learning about trends in your industry and workplace. How do you apply those trends to what you are doing now?

If you are insatiably curious, you will keep asking the questions that will put you ahead of others. While others are recoiling from the stress of change and complaining about how it will impact them, be curious enough to know what is coming technologically and brainstorm how it might help you do your job better so you can stand out more.

If you've fallen behind, you can catch up.

"Regret is an ugly business," Arruda said. "The bad news is that you feel fifteen years behind, but the good news is that you can get caught up quickly. You can build your brand on the Web. Start to build relationships with people in LinkedIn groups rapidly, without having to join a professional association and go to twelve meetings in a row. You can meet fifty new people that you need to know and be successful in one LinkedIn group, and you can start those conversations at any time of the day that is convenient for you. You can make up those fifteen years really quickly. You just need to be uncomfortable because it means getting outside your comfort zone."

Rebranding Is a Slow Boil

When you need to change your brand, see it as a process of evolution, not revolution, he said. You're not going to be the old-timer one day and Mr. or Ms. Innovator the next.

"You need to do it over time. The best way is to look where you engage with the most people who count and to rethink the way you do activities with them. Let's take meetings, for example. We know a lot of people spend between 30 and 50 percent of their time in meetings. In those meetings, there are a lot of people you're looking to influence, the people who work for you, the people you work for, people in other departments who are really important and may be able to do your job. Take that meeting and break it into all its parts. You get an agenda, a reminder, and then a welcome, action items, then a close. Ask yourself how you integrate whatever it is you're trying to change in your brand with each of those action steps. If you want to become more innovative, figure how you can innovate each of those activities and demonstrate how innovative you are through each of them. And if you do that over and over and over, their impressions of you evolve. That's the evolutionary part of it."

Pay attention to your visual brand as well.

You should have current clothes. And notice what people are doing in the office. Are you using your laptop when everyone else is using their phone? Watch what you are doing compared with others because your clothes, surroundings, and tools make an impression.

And while you're spiffing up your image, it's time to stop talking or joking about your age. Arruda says we own our image. We do have control over what we wear and what we say. That made me remember something crisis communication expert Kyla Thompson once stressed to me: don't advertise your age.

Thompson said she asked her son if he'd ever hired anyone her age. Yes, he said, but he didn't contract with her again.

"He said she kept joking about her age, so they kept thinking she was going to retire," Thompson said. "I made the decision instantly to never refer to my age again. Most people do not know how old you really are until you tell them. They don't think about your age until you tell them. A lot of ageism is self-inflicted. A lot."

So don't dilute your brand with it.

If you want to make yourself seem more relevant, get comfortable using the tools that make you more relevant.

You have to swim in your discomfort zone, but the other option is comfortably drowning.

What is so interesting about Arruda's story is that, while being the branding guru onstage, he had to drastically change *his* business plan as the meeting industry changed dramatically.

"Personal branding has moved online, so now I'm kind of a digital branding guy," he said. "I've had to learn all this new stuff. So I've become very fluent in all things digital. It's been frankly an exciting learning curve to become the person who understands the intersection of personal branding in the digital world of social media. At some point, the switch happened."

His big awakening came when he realized corporate clients were more excited about getting their people active online than they were about the personal branding work he was known for. Companies used to be afraid that people would be online wasting time, but now they're working hard to equip them to be successful online.

"I decided to jump in the deep end and just own it," he said. "Now I have content that is relevant to my clients and have the delivery vehicles they are looking for as well. And, for organizations that are slower to move, I am doing the old stuff."

He rebranded.

11

Innovators at Work

I can't really tell you what innovator David Will does for a living because it keeps changing. He is always twisting and turning his original idea until it is even bigger, better, and way more lucrative.

"I don't want to be great," he told me. "If I wait to be great, I'm never going to get anything done. I'm never going to have a business kicking ass. I'll still be sitting there waiting at stage one."

We have plenty to learn from Will and other innovators as we chart our comebacks. These are people who dare to risk huge failures in order to innovate huge successes.

Will fully embraces what LinkedIn founder Reid Hoffman so famously said: "If you are not embarrassed by the first version of your product, you've launched too late."

"Imperfection is just a sign of opportunity in the future," said Will, owner of software company PropFuel. I met him when he owned Peach New Media, a software company that developed a learning platform. "People ask, 'Do you want to be great?' My answer is no! I just want to be good enough to get to the next stage. I want to be great in the big picture, not here in this little thing. I want to be great in the scheme of things."

There is so much in that quote. It gives you, the innovator, a license to be imperfect. The innovator looks around their house and sees flaws in the flooring, and instead of focusing on what's wrong, tells themself, "That's what led us to getting our house done. If we didn't allow any imperfections, we'd still be dealing with contractors a year and a half later."

When Will began his career, one boss said the path to success required that he "Walk faster and smile less." The tech bubble burst, and he was fired from that job, but he knew he wasn't valuable to the company, and he wasn't valuable because he wasn't his true self.

So he became an entrepreneur with this mantra: "Walk slow and smile more." He wants to be happy and authentic, which frees him to try new things.

He dove into business believing that "Good and done is better than perfect."

"I regularly thought, What do I need to change to stay one step ahead? What do I need to change to make this a little bit better?" he said.

One good idea always led to something different, more up-to-date, and more lucrative. He went from selling Web conferencing to managing Web conferencing events to helping organizations create a series of events that populated their library of recordings to helping companies produce events and building a site where they hosted and sold the recordings. Will then realized his company had created a learning management system they could roll out on a regular basis and, instead of managing it for clients and using software to deliver a service, his company would help people create a library with a system that was automated.

He got stronger by hiring good people around him.

Collaborating with others took one idea, morphed it into the next, and sparked the next until Peach New Media grew into a hip company that Will sold for a solid eight figures.

Now he's starting anew with PropFuel.

"What you think you are going to build is very rarely what you are going to end up with," he said. The company is building an automated relationship with customers so there is constant feedback.

It's a startup, and Will sure does love that.

"We have a startup mentality, so we are super agile," he said. Look how quickly his first company changed from one thing into something else that was completely different; then he did it again.

"We started this with the idea of using the technology we had for employee recognition, but it led us down this path where we discovered a huge gap in the way people manage surveys with customers," he said. "We now have campaigns that ask questions over a long period of time—just one or two questions—instead of a big twenty-question, one-time survey. It may be a question a month or a week."

That cements the relationship with customers, and the feedback is valuable.

Will's thirteen-year-old son was starting to run. Will told him the best runners are those who can endure discomfort the longest. It doesn't hurt. It's uncomfortable—unless you are injured, and then it hurts.

"Discomfort is where you grow," he said. "Find something that makes you uncomfortable and you will be on a whole new journey."

He has good advice for those who have hit a wall in their careers.

"Chances are that they stopped innovating," he said. "My guess is, when they were younger, they were evolving and then, it stopped. When you first get a car, you're often in love with it. But, after a while, it just becomes a car, a utility. Same thing can happen with marriages. Oftentimes, people have that happen at work. They get a job, everything is new, but at some point, they lose that drive to keep it fresh. They get into a routine. People resist change. Entrepreneurs thrive in change, crave it, and are searching for change. You grow in that point where you feel discomfort. If you are stuck, get uncomfortable. Repot yourself. When does a plant grow? When you repot it. Challenge yourself to do something you are not used to. That's where you will thrive."

How the Team Works to Innovate

Patrick Burgess is a forty-two-year-old freelance industrial designer and mechanical engineer and the most innovative person I have ever met. He's a professional inventor, and so humble that he'd never boast about his brilliance because he makes it clear that, "It takes a lot of people to bring a product into reality."

"The proper design process is finding a problem, then finding a solution to the problem. Is the inventor the person who discovered the problem or is the inventor the company that wants to go into the specific market or is it me because I'm the one who gets to shape and form the characteristics to the product? I'm not the company owner on any of these, and rarely is it just my idea. There's a problem and we come together to solve the problem, with a lot of people involved in the process."

And yet, what was he doing the day of our interview? Designing a toilet seat that will clean your toilet. And also a kid's scooter. Oh, and an oxygen concentrator and some weight-lifting equipment.

"That's all just today," he said.

In the past, he's designed office furniture, electronics, sporting goods, a lot of medical products, housewares, kitchen items, fashion, footwear, you name it. I've known him for more than a decade and there's always something he is either creating or improving.

The process is long and complicated. It's design, it's engineering, sometimes it's both, sometimes it can't be.

"Kids do it naturally," he said. "You don't have to encourage them at all, at least not my kids. They love to pretend and imagine and make stuff up. My son just asked me, 'What does dinosaur taste like?' Kids have no problem imagining. If you put them in front of a TV, they'll just stare at it. But if you give them something to play with, they'll make up a story and pretend one thing is something else and give you a dog bowl full of blocks and say, 'Here's your soup. Your soup is ready.'"

What inhibits our creativity is that we don't take time to just play and be imaginative, said Burgess.

"We are too busy with our daily stuff."

Everyday life can stand between us and our greatness, he said.

For him, new creations come out of inspiration and research. He has to understand what else is available and figure out the failures in the existing products. He searches for the opportunity to make improvements, and that is where he focuses. In terms of products, the sell point may be better engineering or even a better understanding of the user.

"I'm just looking for different inspiration."

Sometimes, his improvements come by following the rules of design that have existed forever. There's the old rule of thirds, the golden rectangle, symmetry, color balance, balance of repetition, unity, variety, harmony, and all the design rules he learned in college.

He plays with things. If there is too much unity, it's boring. If there is too much variety, it's uncomfortable.

He needs to be aware of what is new, what's selling, what

people like. When he's designing medical equipment, he must think about how the design will look ten years ahead, because the product may well still be in use.

"If this year's hot color is green, I'm not going to make it green," he said. "I'll make it gray because gray always looks nice. Or if it's medical, I'll make it white because white is always going to look nice for a medical product. Whereas, if it is a cell phone case, you have to know what color is trending this year, which Google can tell you."

I asked him what happens professionally as innovators age.

"There are a lot of people much, much older than me who are incredibly relevant and influential," he said. "It just comes down to being good at what you do and continuing to work at it."

He has to stay current because products change every day. He never imagined working on a product that will stick to the end of a golf club to analyze a golf swing or on Bluetooth-chipped devices that track luggage.

"I'm listed as the inventor on hundreds of patents, but it's almost always a true team effort, collaborative. It is usually built upon something that already exists."

He just completed designing an ultralight camping chair that folds up to the size of a bottle and pops up in a matter of seconds.

"Someone was already making ultralight camping chairs, but the setup was a problem," he said. "We had investors who wanted to solve that problem. I invented how it opens, but the way it opens uses some bevel gears—which I didn't invent. I didn't invent the first chair. I definitely didn't invent camping chairs or invent camping. I took a lot of different things and put them together into something that nobody had ever seen before."

So you don't have to be the only one with ideas, and in fact you won't be.

He gave another example. Burgess said a software person invented Bluetooth, but a hardware person had to figure out how to make it real. Years later, someone at an airport didn't know where his suitcase was and got the idea to ask if there was technology to solve that problem.

Investors went to Burgess and wondered what technology could help someone find their suitcase. He had to come up with five options, then figure out what made the most sense, what the battery life would be, how big it would be, and other issues.

A lot of different things came together until there was suddenly a way to check where your suitcase was—via Bluetooth and an app. Burgess was instrumental in designing it, but he always credits others in the process for making the final result because, to him, innovation is all about collaboration.

"The heart of the innovation is finding the problem," he said. "The guy who realized he wanted to know where the suitcase was, he's the important one. Things evolve more than they are created."

Putting Innovative Instincts to Work

I have to tell you about Michelle Brigman.

I felt so sorry for her when she told me she was taking a new position at Dell. It was 2008 and, clearly, she'd been demoted. It sure looked that way to me.

She had been senior operations manager, and suddenly she was going to be in charge of something called "Social Listening and Engagement."

When she explained it to me, she said something about Facebook (which I was just joining) and social media and blog comments, and it all sounded like a bunch of hooey. I wondered who she'd ticked off in senior management.

She was actually onto something very, very big, and her story, like others in this chapter, shows how innovation is the result of asking the right questions and taking a few chances at the right time.

Brigman was one of the first to connect the power of social media with customer relations. She helped build something so significant it impacted millions of consumers. It is now a core marketing strategy of virtually every company in the world.

Dell's customers were talking about the company—a lot. Dell wasn't listening because it didn't know those conversations were happening online.

Brigman had a search done and found that there were tens of thousands of online conversations about the brand:

". . . and we had no idea. They were happening on blogs, on different websites, on technical magazines that might have done product reviews, on Twitter, maybe Facebook. Sometimes they were happening to us directly on our websites. It was all out there.

"I used it to find out what customers actually needed. They were distressed and needed help, and in those forums, they had feedback."

Innovation is often born out of "what if?" And Brigman was asking "what if" at the perfect time.

Her story and the others in this chapter show how different leaders embrace innovation to create something new.

Brigman saw social media and started making calls to find out who knew somebody who knew something about the potential of this new communication. That's what Brigman always does. She asks, "Who do I need to talk to?"

She found a man at Dell who knew a little about it, and he became her teacher. She learned that there were thousands of online posts where people were discussing issues they were having or asking questions. Nobody was monitoring or responding to them. She realized this was a priceless way to learn the real issues customers faced.

It was pretty primitive back then. She'd search keywords or mentions and start organizing the feedback as it would crawl on social media. Depending on what they were talking about, she'd route people to different groups at Dell for action.

Ultimately, that online communication showed employees, designers, and company leadership what was working and what wasn't with Dell's products. It turned customers into real people. The company had tolerated a certain percentage of unknown and unanswered problems because it was just the way things were always done. All of this new instant communication made it possible to know what was really going on out there. It wasn't necessary to sacrifice 1 percent of their customers to unknown problems because, with social media, the problems were no longer unknown.

She still loves Dell but left the company because "It wasn't interesting and new to me anymore. I'm a builder. Once it is a little monotonous, I'm ready to hand over the torch. Then Citi called with building an opportunity, so I went there, and now I am at 7-Eleven. Give me some runway. That's all I need." Brigman is director of customer experience for 7-Eleven and innovating there in a different environment.

The takeaway: to innovate, identify a problem, learn about it, and collaborate to solve it.

12

Don't Let Your Career Manage You

Maureen McGurl hasn't lost her edge—and won't.

She is a trailblazing former C-suite leader who ran HR departments at major corporations, the latest being the Stop & Shop Supermarket Company, before launching Sutton Place HR Consulting in 2008.

McGurl knows how the game is played. She has been there as a trailblazer when she was the only woman on executive leadership teams. She mentored and developed others to join her. Now in a later stage of her career, she thrives because her goal is to stay fresh and relevant so she is always "in the game."

"The world is constantly changing," she said. "You have to be up to date on those changes, concepts, and ideas and adapt to and use them. I used to talk to my teams about the body of knowledge changing every five years or so, but now it might be a year, it might be six months. You have to find ways to stay on top of it. You have to make sure you are staying up to date and relevant so you can live to fight another day."

McGurl networks with this in mind: don't just network. You also need to "net give," and that means doing things for others.

"That giving is really important so you also get."

Also, she said, manage your career. Don't let it manage you.

What do you want to do next? Where do you want to go? Explore those questions, then map out how you are going to get there. That may mean moving up, laterally, or even down. But you are looking for experiences that will help you get to your goal. Don't wait for a company to tell you what your next step should be. Especially now.

"You have to see whether you are in an industry or a job that is under attack now. Is it going to exist for a while? If so, you can track a career for yourself in that world. But you have to ask, 'Am I in an industry that is radically changing and going to disappear?' Then you need to say, 'What is the industry, what is the job I need to be thinking about? Because it's clear my job is not going to exist five years from now.' That means you are being proactive, mapping out where you are going to go. You don't want to be standing there with no plan."

When she launched her consultant business, she would do projects free to gain experience, expanding her portfolio so she could get more work.

"I would do a day's project or do some work to give something of value so they could see the value that could come from me," she said. "That's how I created my consulting business."

She is a master of staying current, and she's someone who has mentored me. I wanted to share her wisdom on achieving relevance because it is so manageable.

First, she said, read, read, read. Read *Fast Company*, the *Harvard Business Review*, *The Wall Street Journal*, white papers, what your CEO is reading . . . just read everything.

"There is so much out there," she said. "As much as we want to read what we enjoy, sometimes we have to read for business to stay current and advance. It is continuing education. You have to know what the hell you're doing."

Staying current is mandatory; it requires effort, and the better your attitude, the better it will work for you.

"Learning can't be work," she said. "Make it fulfilling. It's a mindset. It's a way of life. If it's just a need, it's exhausting. But if it is a thirst, it is invigorating."

At some point, too much information becomes information overload. There is simply too much to read, so McGurl has a great system for staying up on news and insights. She reads excerpts and summaries, skipping full articles unless she needs more depth.

"Pick up *The Wall Street Journal* and look down the left side. You'll see the summary. I read those summaries all the time so that I know what is happening," she said. "If I need to know more, I read the article. If you read the *Harvard Business Review* cover to cover, page by page, you'll never have time to do anything else. But read the summaries in the front of the magazine to capture the essence of the idea."

Then, talk about what you are reading and learning. Reference it in conversations. That is how you advertise you are current.

McGurl doesn't advertise how old she is, although she is beyond sixty-five.

"My age has never bothered me," she said. "I am what I am and I have earned it."

She doesn't broadcast it, though, because she still wants to work and be engaged.

"If you begin to think of yourself as old, that is what you are," she said. "But age can be held against you. People might automatically wonder, are you with it? Are you current? Do you have a good sense of what is happening in this world? It's an issue for men and women, but women's ages are held against them more. Men are held to a different standard. They are seen to age with grace."

McGurl knows there is true age bias in organizations and in people, but counters that with, "Poor me isn't going to get you anywhere. There is this big world that often puts roadblocks in front of us. Stay fresh, stay current so you can remove those roadblocks and win."

Good advice whether you are still in your job, have lost it, or are returning to the workplace after an absence.

13

Bye-Bye, Dinosaur, Hello, Innovator

Innovation = job security.

Period.

This is an era of innovation, and the innovators rule because they are driving the change that is coming. Innovation is valuable, and it's exactly what companies want. Remember all those leaders saying that they want to know where you stand on the runway into the future? Well, one class of highly sought-after professionals refuses to stand on the runway. They race forward on it, trying to identify and solve future problems. These are the innovators.

You may think you are not an innovator, but consider this: you were actually a creative genius and master innovator when you were a little kid. You just unlearned all those skills when you stopped playing with pretend people and coming up with fantastical play stories. Years ago, NASA hired scientists George Land and Beth Jarman to find a way to gauge the creative potential in people. They designed a scientific test to measure "divergent thinking." When they tested 1,600 five-year-olds, they were shocked to learn that 98 percent of the kids scored as creative geniuses.

Five years later, they went back to the same children and were flabbergasted that only 30 percent scored the same. Another five years later, 12 percent made that grade.

When Land and Jarman tested adults, only 2 percent were creative geniuses.

Children have healthy imaginations that allow them to see without constraint. Adults have been fed so much negativity and reality that we stop imagining what we can't see. We live in the realm of rules and constraint, which keeps us from being players in a change-driven workplace.

It's time to figure out how to liberate your inner five-year-old. Open up. See things with fresh eyes. Be positive. Just play with what is in front of you.

Are innovators born? Or can they be trained and cultivated?

I once thought you had to be born to innovate, but after studying user innovation in an MIT class, I learned that each of us can innovate on our own. Innovation is simple. You just solve a problem that you have. That's where you find the need.

Dropbox started when university student Drew Houston kept forgetting his USB memory stick. He created cloud storage for the masses, and now I can see this chapter from anywhere with my account.

GoPro started when Nick Woodman wanted an affordable camera that would take great action photos. I've used mine diving, kayaking, cycling, whitewater rafting, and hiking.

Both innovators saw an unmet need and dared to figure out how to meet it.

I was surprised how simple the user innovation process is.

In the MIT class, we were assigned to come up with ten problems or obstacles in our lives that needed solutions, then home in on one of them. We had to study our strengths and skills, then look at our list of problems to determine which would be the best one to focus on solving, based on our skill set. Then we had to plan how we'd launch it into the world and if we'd sell or license it. By the time I finished the class, I had a really good idea that would be worth pursuing if I weren't so happy doing what I am doing. But the point is, I had no idea that I knew how to initiate this, and now I do.

If you think you are not innovative, rethink.

Lessons from the Masters

Let's take a couple of quick lessons from the two greats, Steve Jobs and Thomas Edison.

Lesson 1: Steve Jobs, founder of Apple

1. "Simple can be harder than complex: You have to work hard to get your thinking clean to make it simple. But it's worth it in the end because once you get there, you can move mountains."
2. "Creativity is just connecting things. When you ask creative people how they did something, they feel a little guilty because they didn't really do it, they just saw something. It seemed obvious to them after a while. That's because they were able to connect experiences they've had and synthesize new things."
3. "Stay hungry, stay foolish."

Lesson 2: Thomas Edison, inventor of the light bulb that revolutionized home electricity, the phonograph, motion picture camera, and more

1. "Negative results are just what I want. They're just as valuable to me as positive results. I can never find the thing that does the job best until I find the ones that don't."

2. "Just because something doesn't do what you planned it to do doesn't mean it's useless."

3. "Many of life's failures are people who did not realize how close they were to success when they gave up."

4. "Our greatest weakness lies in giving up. The most certain way to succeed is always to try just one more time."

You don't have to be the next Steve Jobs. You don't even have to be the most innovative person in the office. You just need to be *more* innovative. Take other people's ideas and come up with a few tweaks. Innovation is one part creativity and one part vision. Your creativity sparks the idea; your vision manifests it.

Learn the processes that will make you *more* innovative so you stand out for asking the questions and coming up with partial answers that make you a valuable player in the development process. Don't leave it to others to design the future. Start contributing to it yourself.

It's Not Too Late to Learn This

If you've spent your life working in cubicles among professionally dressed, well-behaved people, you may be uncomfortable when you first encounter one of the new, innovative workspaces that are filled with wild artwork, toys, open spaces, and people at stand-up desks or desks with treadmills. Bright colors, couches, pool tables. The modern office runs so counter to the rigid, predictable reality we have known all along, but it has changed in an effort to liberate workers from the rules that have kept their ideas in check with the status quo.

Companies now want their people relaxed and comfortable so they can *think*. Open spaces where workers interact and collaborate became idea generators.

Dive in. Open up. Learn. Give yourself permission to have stupid ideas, because you can't come up with something great if you aren't free to come up with something really dumb.

Ants Don't Sleep

I once attended a writers' conference where famed novelist Tom Robbins stood in front of an auditorium packed with at least three hundred people and said, "The second sentence is as important as the first. I'm going to give you the first sentence and then you write a second sentence for it. The first sentence is, 'Ants don't sleep.' Now, write down your second sentence."

Everybody wrote down their second sentence.

He then started with the first person on the right in the first row. "What is your second sentence?" The guy read a sentence. Then Robbins asked the person in the next seat, "What is yours?" The woman read hers. The two stories were now completely different. Robbins kept going down the row. Ten people into it, you could see there were ten stories.

Unfortunately, he did this with the *entire* auditorium. After ten people, we got the point. It seemed to me that Robbins was not prepared for this conference and found this cheesy exercise to waste an hour of our time.

But it taught me one thing. Three hundred people can come up with three hundred answers. Many weren't great, but some were worth developing. So when you look at a problem, realize that there are many, many possibilities to solve it. Many won't be great, some will be terrible, but there will be a few winners.

Several years ago, I started writing a novel and did what most people do. I started, wrote a few pages, then stopped, then started, wrote a little more, then stopped, then started . . .

I kept stalling out until I found a book called *No Plot, No Problem,* and within a few weeks, I finished the novel. Here's what the book said that liberated me to finish: every day, you have to write a certain number of words. It could be five hundred or a thousand or even five thousand. But you make the commitment and you have to write that many words. It doesn't matter if what you write is awful. You just have to sit down and write what you have promised to write. You can edit or delete when you have finished.

I combined that advice with something a professor once taught me: never edit what you are writing until you've finished a draft or you will never finish that draft. I absolutely believe that. Millions of aspiring writers get stuck rewriting the first paragraph, first page, first chapter, and never get to chapter 2.

So if you free yourself for creative thinking and idea generation, you have tremendous power to innovate when you realize:

You have permission to come up with a bunch of ideas that totally stink. Unless you are free to do that, you will inhibit your thought process. Somewhere in the middle of the garbage is going to be a diamond. You have to recognize it, polish it off, and present it right.

Quantity over quality at first. Don't worry about improving any of your ideas until you have finished brainstorming. Get in the habit of generating many ideas so you will get used to the creative process.

Don't Go It Alone

What would the Rolling Stones be without Keith? Or Mick? Both are phenomenal artists, but they are their greatest together. Half the time, they don't even like each other. But they know that great bands are great because they band together.

When innovating, you may find your real greatness in collaboration.

Yes, you have to share the credit, but that's just teamwork. As you develop as an innovator, realize there are two ways of doing it: solo or with others. Working with others is faster and more productive. It also tags you as a team player and shows you work with other generations.

1. It begins with relationships and communication. Sometimes a multimillion-dollar idea pops into your head, but more often it is born out of a conversation that twists and pivots and finally leads to that magic moment when somebody says, "Hey, what if . . ." You can see your colleagues as competitors (which they often are), but they also are your most valuable collaborators. Develop relationships that welcome an open mind and crazy ideas.

2. Erase the hierarchy in your mind and listen to everybody. Find people who don't know what they are supposed to think or who don't react the way they think they are supposed to react. They don't have the same assumptions and prejudices that are built into your perspective.

3. Outsiders and newcomers have fresh views. Why not ask your admins, interns, and new employees what they think?

4. Don't be so specific with your questions that you miss out on some of the more creative answers. Listen more than you talk. You don't need to demonstrate how smart you are or offer solutions. Ask questions and limit your instructions. Consider the quality of the idea, not the rank or expertise of the idea generator.

Creative thinking takes a great deal of confidence because others will hear what you've come up with and either like or dislike what you've offered. The fear that you will sound stupid or be rejected can be crippling. But it is all part of the process.

Innovation = creativity + risk.

Innovation = job security.

Examine, Disengage, Brainstorm, Scrutinize, Test, Launch

Ask yourself:

> What exactly am I trying to solve here?
> What is the end result I am trying to achieve?
> What isn't working with it now?
> What would be the absolute worst solution?
> Does knowing that give me a new framework for the best solution?
> What would I do if I had an unlimited budget to solve this?
> What will it look like in five years? Ten?

Once you have that down, give your brain a breather. Meditate, do yoga, run, sleep—do something that pulls you out of the intensity of creative focus and just breathe.

Then go back at it. Get with your creative partners and push each other to come up with new solutions—as many as possible. Then go through them and scrutinize which ones are worth keeping and which are worth tossing.

Move through the test phase and launch knowing that you are never really done with anything. You might be done "for now," but the moment will come when something needs to be tweaked or tossed, and then you start again.

When you come up with an idea that you believe in, really believe in it. Have the courage to carry it forward. Remember, if you don't carry your ideas forward, you will be choosing the company of all the other cowards who are too afraid to stand out.

If you want to be valued (and employed), you have to brand yourself as an idea person. Someone who is creative and innovative and brave about it.

Be brilliant.

And be confident.

Persist

There are millions of creative geniuses whose visions are never realized and whose finances are in tatters. Why? Because they quit too soon.

Innovation is a process of hit or miss. Endless hit or miss. Excruciating hit or miss.

"The idea isn't right."

"That's a little better."

"Closer, but not quite there."

"Hmmm. That is interesting. Tell me more."

"Let's try it."

"Ugh, that didn't work at all. Now what are you going to do?"

"That's no good. Try again."

"Hmmm. What if . . ."

"Okay, I like that, let's try it."

"Blech. Not right this time, either. Try again . . ."

"You're *still* working on that? Okay, can you remind me about it again?"

"Hmmm."

"Hey, that is interesting."

"Wow! THIS IS GREAT. Let's do it."

I always remember: You never know how close you are to turning the corner until you turn the corner.

And if it doesn't work, you learn. If you don't fail a little, you are nowhere near your limits.

If you want to clamp your creative valve shut, refuse to fail. That's all it takes. Fear of embarrassment, fear of rejection, fear of failure. You can intimidate yourself into a corner where you only have safe ideas.

Safe ideas are great when the status quo is strong enough to take care of whatever change is coming. The status quo is not a safe place for people who want long-term, viable careers.

You will never win if you are too afraid to lose.

Great ideas can bomb. If you accept that from the beginning, you can depersonalize the fallout. Most importantly, when something is not working, you know how to sound the alarm and then rapidly recover with an adjustment or exit. Remember what Edison said about failing: *"Our greatest weakness lies in giving up. The most certain way to succeed is always to try just one more time."*

In 1890, Edison told *Harper's Monthly* magazine, "I speak without exaggeration when I say that I have constructed three thousand different theories in connection with the electric light, each one of them reasonable and apparently to be true. Yet only in two cases did my experiments prove the truth of my theory."

Do you have the persistence and stamina to try something and fail three thousand times? What about just three?

Our only defense against irrelevance is to deliver. The only way to deliver is to do what all the other idea people are doing, whether they are ten years younger, twenty years younger, or even thirty years younger. When they hit the wall, they try again.

There's a meme I love of an old, mixed-breed dog getting hit in the head with the tennis ball he was trying to catch. The huge caption says, "FAIL!"

But I love it because I know that the next time someone threw a ball to him, he tried just as hard to catch it.

That's what we have to do. Keep running after the ball. Sooner or later, we will catch it.

Remember: innovation = job security.

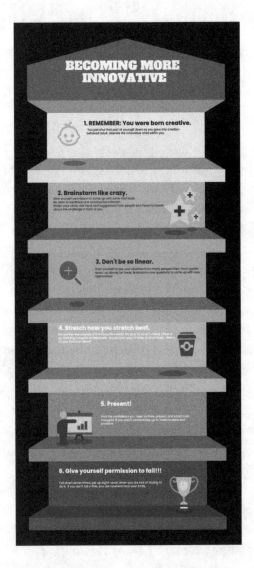

14

Stop Networking Like a Wimp

Flying to Boston, I sat next to a man who just had to show me the picture he'd received from home of the mass destruction left behind after his golden retriever went on a rampage in the garbage. I'm a dog person, and we started sharing stories. I told him my name, he told me his, and soon I found out he was head of sales for an insurance company, and he learned I was a speaker and author. By the time I got off the flight, he wanted me as his keynote for the annual sales conference in Las Vegas. That is my kind of networking.

But wait, there's more. I'd been on the road for so long and desperately needed my nails done, so I stopped at a salon before my speech. While at the drying table, I befriended a woman who was senior vice president at a national financial services company. Within a year, I was hired to speak at her company. We're still friends.

Bam! Boom! Kapow!

That is the kind of networking I like. I would much rather make friends at a nail salon than try to network a roomful of strangers at a cocktail reception or conference where everybody is doing the same. I have gotten business by talking to strangers on airplanes, in buffet lines, while cycling, on Facebook, and even at a parade. The conversations that mattered most involved dogs, kids, relationships, trips, embarrassing moments, television shows, mutual friends, the Who, and other "important" matters. I'm interested in people and genuinely enjoy making friends, and that leads to the relationships that lead to more business.

The reason I don't like networking at conferences is that I am a tad shy. It's much easier to speak in front of two thousand people onstage than talk to a bunch of strangers at a networking event. I still do the reception networking, but I network every day—wherever I happen to be.

If you do it right, you can easily call, text, or email the people in your network, admit you need help, say what you need, ask specifically for what you want from them, check back to see if they have delivered, and keep checking in until they have.

I did my best networking during the COVID-19 lockdown. Yes, while everybody was stuck at home, I set up mega video calls where power players in my network got together for a glass of wine. The beauty of it was that I knew nobody was doing anything, everybody was available, and most of these type A power-hitters were bored out of their minds. I had multiple calls with ten to fifteen people on them, and all those people were usually so busy they could *never* get their schedules to align. I just set a time, told them who I was inviting, and sent the link. I had 98 percent attendance, every single time. Those video calls were so important to all of us, giving us a place to connect, commiserate, and laugh. The friendships deepened, and so did the value of our network.

Few people truly leverage their networks. They float through networking events, shaking the right hands, reciting their memorized elevator pitches, exchanging business cards, and sending bland follow-up emails. But they never truly create or leverage a network that will deliver.

They know "It's not what you know but *who* you know," so they try to know the right people. But they fail to find the connecting point that turns a contact into an ally or, even better, a friend. Meaningful connections are why people close deals, get hired, win promotions, and avoid layoffs. They are often what stands between winning and losing.

It is not enough to develop a network based solely on professional standing and influence. It is much more important that you know I love dogs, adventure, and Thursday-night television than it is that you know what I do for a living.

People help their friends! That is not to say that they don't help people they meet at receptions, luncheons, on LinkedIn, or through email introductions. They do. I do. I do have a number of contacts that are strictly professional. But I always try to find the connecting point that elevates someone from an acquaintance to a friend.

People *really* like to help their friends, and they do it with much more exuberance and regularity than helping acquaintances or strangers. They want their friends to be happy and successful. Helping friends is a benefit of their success. They also trust that friends they recommend will deliver.

So, as you network, find ways to be liked and loved. Find out where people grew up, what they watch on television, what sports they follow, where they went to college, started their careers, how they met their significant others—I don't care. There is *always* a connecting point.

If you do this at an event, strategize by doing online research in advance on some of the people you are likely to meet so you have good conversation starters. There are connecting points everywhere, even if you start with, "I liked the article you posted."

Don't act starry-eyed or intimidated. You are as good as anybody else. You may not have as many accomplishments, but we're all people. Don't bow down. Nobody belongs on a pedestal.

Getting time with a person of influence is a tremendous opportunity to advertise your skills, what you can do, and how you might work together. That is why you have an elevator speech. But if you have a chance to go beyond that, that's where you find the magic. Allow them to talk about themselves, because people still love, love, love to do that.

I know someone who met the CEO of a major corporation at a party. She found him utterly obnoxious, but when she mentioned that they both came from the same small town in Connecticut, they started reminiscing about their teachers, the mayor, the local grocery store, and where everybody used to go to make out. They bonded.

What Good Is a Network You Can't Leverage?

Pride is an expensive commodity.

If you are too proud to ask for help, you won't get help. And yet asking may be the only thing standing between you and the opportunity that solves everything.

It can be especially hard for people facing comeback career challenges to admit they need help because their self-esteem may already be fragile and their pride gets in the way. But even the greatest performers with the most experience can still fall prey to a changing workplace or jerks in the office or a life circumstance that requires a career change or a pause. Your best route to new opportunity is through the people who may intimidate you. Even in moments when it is hard to believe in yourself, you must. If you don't believe in you, no one else will, either.

Never in history has it been both easier and harder to enlist other people in the cause of your success. Easy, because it is so easy to find and reach people. Hard, because the easiness of access means people are besieged by inquiries. But there are certain ways to stand out and take the steps that will propel you ahead of the others.

Networking Is Both Strategic and Accidental

You should know who you need to know. If you are trying to break into a company, look up the key players. Check LinkedIn to see if you know people who know those people. Study them and figure out where you might meet them or who might provide an introduction. That's strategic.

What is accidental (and fabulously helpful) is when you are with friends who meet up with those influential people, and your friends casually make the introduction. You start with an advantage because you know someone they know (and hopefully like), so that means you must be worth listening to.

Being strategic means going to networking groups and industry meetings. Be there. Meet people. People at networking groups are also trying to expand their networks, so don't just advertise that you need something. Talk to them and find out what they need that you might be able to help with. Try to make friends.

Another thing: just because you meet somebody who isn't "there" yet, it doesn't mean they won't be "there" tomorrow. Be friends with everybody.

Cold Approaches

Networking used to come down to face-to-face meetings and introductions. Now you can network with senior executives on the other side of the world.

Neela Montgomery, CEO of Crate and Barrel, wanted to connect with a CEO of another company that was working with something new that she wanted to know about. She reached out on LinkedIn, asked if the person was willing to talk about it, and then they met.

"That was a cold electronic connection," she said. "These days, people don't have the hang-ups they used to have on that. This is the Facebook generation. It's a little uncomfortable the first time you do it, but it is totally normal in this day and age."

But that was CEO to CEO. Would that work if someone tried that from the outside?

"I don't take sales calls, because that is a nightmare," Montgomery said. "I had somebody approach me from an innovative software company. They had an idea, so I set up a call with them and now they are going to come and visit my office. There is definitely a way to access leaders that didn't exist before. They wouldn't have gotten through the reception or personal assistant, but now they can access me on LinkedIn."

How should we make an approach?

"Obviously, if they write horribly, I'll notice. If they write too elegantly or elaborately, I would tend not to read it. Being punchy and succinct has become very important. I guess we all have to write in headlines these days," Montgomery said.

Well put.

Some leaders are open to it, some aren't, because they are besieged by too many inquiries.

"I get so many of those," said Tom Greco, CEO of Advance Auto Parts. "It's too much. I respond to emails from customers—I want those dealt with by sundown. But I probably get thirty other inquiries a day that I delete and press Block Sender. When you have LinkedIn and you connect with some of these people, they immediately want to sell something. If it is somebody with a unique background, I might pay attention, but typically, I don't."

Cracking the Email Code

Outside of LinkedIn, consider email. I do this all the time.

I can usually figure out a CEO or senior executive's email address on the Internet. I start by searching for the name of the CEO. Once I have the name, I search for that person's name and the words "email address" because a lot of them have been exposed on the Web. If not, I look at the company website and try to ascertain the format of the company's emails. I will often check the press area, because there is usually an email for the media contact and the address after the @ sign is usually where most company emails go. Then, if you see how other emails are formatted, you just copy that with the right letters from the CEO's name.

Here is a made-up example: Jane Adams is CEO of WXYZ-Corp. I go to their website and see emails are sent to first initial then last name @wxyzcorp.com. So hers would be jadams@wxyzcorp.com. If I can't see the exact format, I guess and it is usually either j_adams@wxyzcorp.com or j.adams@wxyzcorp.com or jane.adams@wxyzcorp.com or Jane_adams@wxyzcorp.com. I then email all those addresses. Often, three bounce back and one works. Then, I am in!

So when you do it, try the same formats and substitute your contact's name or initials. This works for me almost every time. Sometimes, the executive reads his or her own emails. Other times, I hear back from someone in the executive office.

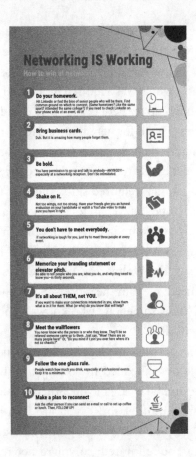

Be Proactive

It is certainly possible to build a network when you are struggling and trying to stage your comeback. It is much easier to maintain an already active network that you can tap into whenever you need something. So as you do this, make a commitment to keeping it active and viable. A good network is a support system that fills your world with talented, smart people. A good network helps you quickly deploy the troops, brainstorm, and make things happen. Always continue to build on it, nurture it, connect with it, and plan to leverage it when you need it.

I interviewed a woman who left her job to raise her kids and was out of the workplace for fifteen years before trying to stage her comeback. By that time, her company had been acquired by another company, which was acquired by another. Her references didn't want to stand up for her because they could barely remember her, much less vouch for her abilities. Her skills were so outdated (even though she insisted they were relevant) that she was asking people who barely remembered her to say she'd be a good candidate for a job that required skills she didn't have. You can see the problem. If she'd stayed in touch, they could have told her what she needed to do to update her skills and, in mentoring her, become a resource when it came time to help get her hired.

Karen Stuckey, the Walmart senior vice president, summed up what you need in your network: "Somebody that knows somebody will know somebody who knows somebody."

That is networking.

You need that network in place at all times instead of getting too comfortable or embedded in a company that you assume will always love and take care of you, Stuckey said.

"If you don't build networks, you are in a bad spot when that happens," she said. "A) You're blindsided. B) You don't have a plan. C) You're injured, so you're not responding productively. You're responding from a point of hurt and anger, hurt or surprise. You can't really think clearly about what your next step is."

Jill Smart is an expert on getting hired. She retired as chief human resources officer for Accenture before becoming president of the National Academy of Human Resources. She laid out the strategy that is most helpful for getting on track.

"Find organizations that somebody might participate in, whether on boards or civic groups or industry groups," she said. "If you can, get to just one person and say, 'Can you help me make sure that HR sees this?' You have to be creative. Maybe you don't know anybody in the organization where you want to work, but you may know somebody who knows somebody."

You aren't inconveniencing people if you present the case that you are an incredible hire.

"Companies love getting good referrals," she said. "It saves them money. They want their employees referring people."

Do you want to count on a computer that is going to sort through hundreds or thousands of applications to decide you are the one who must, must, must get the job?

"You can't depend on the algorithm to bring you to the top of the pile," said China Widener, a principal at Deloitte who is a strategy and operations leader, as well as a force in diversity and inclusion. "That's just not how it works. You've got to get to the humans. The machine is going to look for certain kinds of words and phrases, and certain kinds of outcomes. But it's not going to judge you. You have to utilize the network you have to get to the network you want, and that is about creating relationships."

Do that while working, socializing, and volunteering.

"Know where the people in that profession spend their time, then get connected," Widener said. Engage with people for the purpose of acquiring the information you need to know or have about an industry. They get an understanding of who you are by the questions you ask. You start to build those relationships, those connections, and you can move to a place where they are willing to then share opportunities that might otherwise not be publicly known because you've developed a personal relationship."

Getting LinkedIn

Turning a contact into a connection makes this social marketing platform one of the most powerful tools in your arsenal. It's one thing to reach out and add a contact, but to build a relationship? That takes a little effort. Once you create a two-way dialogue, you share ideas and articles and become more comfortable asking for help.

So if you have hundreds of contacts on LinkedIn, big deal. That's easy. If you have fifty connections that will help you achieve and move forward, that's gold.

First, have a professional photo taken. I know someone who is so uncomfortable with how the years have aged her, she's using a forty-year-old photo. For real. You need a good, current photo. If you don't look perfect, nobody does. If you look haggard, well, that's why we have professional makeup and Photoshop.

Read up on how to create a profile that is well-written and intriguing. Get recommendations from people who can vouch for you.

Don't use it in a way that repels the people you are trying to enlist. Speaker David Avrin, author of multiple books, including *It's Not Who You Know, It's Who Knows You!* posted this on-point rant on Facebook:

> LinkedIn is being ruined. 99% of people who ask to connect with me on LinkedIn, pitch me their business immediately. Yuck! To be clear, I will never, ever do business with someone who pitches me blind on LinkedIn. Not just because of the ludicrous nature of expecting a response from an unsolicited pitch, but because you've said something clear about your level of business sophistication. By your actions, you're saying: "I don't know what I'm doing. I am clueless about human behavior and business basics." To be honest, I can't be associated with professionals who don't understand business. And if they don't understand their business, how could they possibly help me with mine?

Your approach has to be quick, direct, and impressive. It should be clear that you are not sending the same inquiry to multiple people. And don't ramble. Three great sentences are a million times better than six good paragraphs and ten million times better than ten rambling paragraphs. Make your case, make it individualized, sound smart, let them know what you want, and then wrap it up.

Widener, from Deloitte, really summed it up for me.

Widener is a strategy and operations leader. If you are cold emailing her, make sure it is about something that is going to trigger her interest. Maybe it is about something she posted, or something she's commented on.

"Make sure you understand the person on the other side so it is likely to trigger interest for them," she said.

"You've got to make it about a topic they care about at that time. There are many topics I care about, but I don't care about all of them in the same window of time. Find the right time and the right topic. You have to get my attention in the 3.4 seconds that I am scanning the message list. The first thing I scan for is whether I know the name. Then the subject matter. If the subject gets to me, I am going to read the first three sentences. I am not reading anything after three sentences. Then I am going to decide in that moment: save it and read it later, trash can it, or read it now? Remember you are asking someone to stop what they are doing, whatever that is, and to focus on you for the next forty-five seconds. That's what you're actually asking somebody to do when you are reaching out that way. There has to be a compelling reason, if you think about it, for me to disrupt the flow of my day to bring into it something I hadn't counted on."

Some career guides suggest that you send a personal note when trying to connect with someone, and that's quite polite. However, I get so many requests, I never read those notes. I just accept, which adds up to plenty of contacts, but not many connections. I just checked my LinkedIn mail and saw ten notes from strangers I took as contacts. All of them have asked me for phone time. Which means none are going to get it. Far better to listen to how William Arruda advises you to handle LinkedIn.

Arruda is the best-known personal branding guru around. He is also a master of turning LinkedIn contacts into personal connections.

"What is it that you are considering doing next? There's a group for that," he said. "If you're in social media marketing, there is a group. If you're in blockchain, there's a group. If you're in financial analysis, there's a group. It doesn't matter what you do, there is a group for it and they are talking about what's coming next in those groups. They post a knowledge base that is all about what is relevant in today's market. You search on the keywords of what it is you want to do next and you join those groups and spend a little bit of time just lurking, figuring out how the group works, who are the people who share the most content, who are the people whose point of view you really connect with, who are the people whose job you wish you had, and then start to connect with these people. It's quite a welcoming community and I think it's really easy to do. You can't make a mistake. Nothing bad can happen. There's only an upside."

There is a serendipity factor in online networking because, while you are looking for others, you don't know who's looking for someone like you. The trick is to be as visible as possible so they can find you.

"Opportunities come to me if I am really visible online," he said. "I'm writing a new book because the publisher was connected to me through someone else in the online community."

It is important to have a hugely diverse network because

opportunity can come from people who have nothing to do with what you do.

"It could be the cashier at the Dollar General," he said. "Those second-level connections are really powerful and give you valuable perspective. If everyone you know is exactly like you, it will be hard to get the perspectives you need to move forward. First, you build your competency, you learn things, you build a community. Then, the more visible you are and engaged you are, the more opportunities come to you."

Arruda looks at what people post, and if a given post makes him want to connect with that person, he comments and says, "Thanks a lot, I'm really glad you posted this. I'd love to connect with you to talk to you about _____.

"It doesn't feel slimy, it puts the ball in their court, and if they want to reach out to me and we have a connection, it's great," he said. "They almost always do because people love when you comment on their stuff. You might have ten thousand people view your article, but only six comments happen. The whole point of it is to have a discussion and engagement."

Create Your Own Instant Power Network

I once strategized how to create a tremendous network while at lunch with a friend. The next time we met, we were to bring a mentor or person of influence. The next time, the people of influence brought their mentors or people of influence. The time after that, those people brought their mentors. We did it for six rounds of dinners and met some really great people who were interested in meeting others they could help. These were all local people, and it was a powerhouse experience.

So easy, so obvious. Yet few people ever do it.

You already have a network. But take a moment to figure out

how to use your network to combine with your network's network.

Getting important people together in the same room can be difficult. Technology lets you do video chats with multiple people at once. Do it! I have hosted "Wine and FaceTime" for years. Waaaay before my super-networking video sessions during the pandemic lockdown.

When you do this with others, there comes a moment when you all start to see things click together. When one person needs a favor and a phone call is made to someone else who knows someone and then, POOF! It is handled. Those are great moments.

The Introvert's Guide to Networking

Rachel Johnson is a true introvert and, because she built her career in the unstable newspaper industry, has found herself job hunting twice in the past few years. She knows networking is critical, but for her it is excruciating.

"It is terrifying," she said. "I am an introvert of the highest degree and I don't do well talking to strangers in groups. It causes me anxiety. I try to put myself in uncomfortable positions, I build myself up and say, 'You can do it, you can do it.' Then I get there and all I want to do is run and hide. Networking is not an easy thing for an introvert. My network is very small because I am an introvert. Luckily I have a very good group of friends; even though it is a small group, it is a good group."

She went to a conference and, fortunately, ran into someone she knew, so she sat with her. Everyone was instructed to turn around and introduce themselves to the people behind and next to them.

"I was very uncomfortable," she remembered. "I get shaky and the words don't come out of my mouth right."

My heart goes straight to her.

Like Johnson, I am an introvert. I have learned a few tricks on how introverts can network.

1. You don't have to do your networking at big events. If you do target networking and either get the right introduction from someone else or reach out via email or LinkedIn, you may be able to do coffee one-on-one, or meet remotely if you are approaching opportunities far from your immediate area.

2. Do your homework. Especially for a one-on-one meeting, you need to know more than the person's title. You should try to know something personal as well. And, as you prepare for a networking event, you can prepare in advance by looking up the people who will be there, studying their backgrounds, and having some idea of what you want to say when you meet them.

3. Bring someone with you to networking events. This is an icebreaker because you can introduce yourselves together or one can introduce the other person. Doing so is generally very welcome for someone who is standing there alone.

4. Be authentic. If you are quiet, it is who you are. It isn't going to work if you come out like some backslapping doofus. Your true self is still your own best asset.

5. Listen to the other person and ask questions instead of doing the talking. It's usually more appreciated when you are more interested than interesting.

6. You don't have to meet everybody in the room. Try to come out with three or four good connections if that's all you can handle.

7. Follow up. Add these new people on LinkedIn and

your other social media outlets. Send a quick email to say you are glad you met, forward an interesting article, ask the person to coffee or lunch—whatever. Do *something* to continue the relationship.

8. Follow up again. Don't be a pest. Just stay on the radar.
9. Use LinkedIn. Comment on their posts. Forward interesting articles.
10. Be bold. Ask for a lunch or coffee meeting.

Conversation Starters

If you aren't sure what to say when you are out networking, fear not. Much in this next section is not original. Most are from online posts from people who have found the way to break the ice while networking.

When starting a conversation:

- "Hi. I don't think we've met before. I'm . . ."
- "Hi, I don't know too many people here, so I wanted to introduce myself. I'm [name] and I work at [company]."
- "Great shoes!" (or tie/hair/handbag/suit)
- "I think we both know [insert name] . . ."
- "So, what do you do?"
- "It's my first time here and I'm trying to meet a few people. Mind if I start with you? I'm . . ."
- "Have you tried the little egg rolls? Wow!"
- "How's your day going?"
- "I'll be honest, the only person I know here is the bartender, and I just met him two minutes ago. Mind if I introduce myself?"
- "Where are you from? Have you lived in the area long? Where do you work?"

When approaching a group of people:

- "I just wanted to join in and introduce myself."
- "Hi, everyone. Do you mind if I squeeze in? I'm . . ."
- "Hi. Room for one more?"

Extracting yourself from the conversation:

- "Well, it has been so good to talk. How might I help you in the future?"
- "It's nice to meet you. It seems like we have a lot in common. Can I send you a LinkedIn invitation?"
- "I've really enjoyed meeting you. I'd enjoy getting together for lunch. Are you game?"
- "I'd enjoy talking with you again. Can I get your card?"

Following Up After Meeting

I often come back from an event with a stack of business cards. Because I must, I will write every single person I've met. I realize that they also came back with a stack of cards, as did every other person at the event. Because of that, there will be many hundreds of emails flying back and forth.

That first contact after a meeting is mandatory, but it often gets lost with many other emails or contacts. Regardless, you have to do it. Mention something interesting from your meeting that will help the person remember who you are. Maybe you connected on some common personal ground and can bring up your kids or your cat or how you both love eating at Red Lobster. Whatever.

Or maybe you came out of the conversation with something you can offer to do for the person; it is always best to give before you get. If you help others first just because you are nice, friendships start to form and the give-and-take becomes a genuine connection. I've had people send me funny cartoons, articles, and dog memes. Some remind me about a conversation about cycling or mutual friends or that they grew up near where I live. When they remind me, I don't feel guilty for having forgotten who they are, which I frequently do, because I have met too many people at the event.

True connections form when your follow-up has continued beyond that first obligatory email. Every so often, find an excuse to pass along something of interest or use to the person. Or something funny.

Don't Ask, Don't Get

So often, we hesitate asking for help because we don't want to put the other person out or make them feel uncomfortable. But if I called you and asked for a favor, you'd probably do it, right?

It makes us feel good to help other people.

Sometimes we are doing people favors in order to ask for favors; sometimes there is no payback expected. Successful people appreciate that their success puts them in a position to help others.

Competitors may or may not help you. I live in Dunedin, a quaint Florida town that became great because, back when there were literally tumbleweeds in the streets, the handful of local restaurant owners figured out that they would be more successful by making sure everyone else was successful. That would make the town attractive, which would draw more people to come here. They cooperated instead of competed. They called it "cooperatition," and that is an epic approach to success. We used to have one brewery in town, and now we seem to be adding another one every month. Instead of the owners of the Dunedin Brewery feeling threatened, they realized more beer meant more success. Many restaurants get their beer brewed by the Dunedin Brewery. All these competitive people helped bring the town a thriving nightlife and community instead of tumbleweeds.

So you actually might get help from your competitors.

If not, there is always someone else doing something similar who can and will help. I have a friend who planned to open a smoothie shop and was rebuffed by a local competitor.

"So what?" I laughed. "Contact a smoothie shop in some other town. I think there are one or two million of them!"

She visited her sister in another state and went to every smoothie shop in town to talk to their owners and learn their stories and suggestions. There's always a way.

Just ask.

"Women tend not to ask as directly for help as men," said Margaret M. Keane, CEO of Synchrony Financial. "We tend to skirt around it. If you are seeking career help, seek someone who is going to sponsor you, not just pass the résumé on. Get someone who will pick up the phone. I would hope we'd all be brave enough to say, 'You know this person. Can you pick up the phone and call this person for me?' You can even say, 'Look, I may be a long shot for the job, but I think that, if I got in and was able to talk to the person face to face, I could have an impact. Can you get them to at least meet with me or have a cup of coffee?'"

Busy people are inundated with requests for help, so be mindful of that. But ASK! And follow up. I am constantly getting requests for help. My stock answer is, "Hey, I am slammed right now. Do you mind following up in two weeks?"

If they follow up, I know they are serious.

Do you know how many people follow up?

Very, very few.

Those are the ones I want to help.

Be Specific. Go Guerilla.

Don't just ask for help. If you need help . . .

ASK.

Specifically, clearly.

Directly.

ASK.

I know that can be very, very uncomfortable, but it must be done. I have sent résumés along to friends who are wonderful people but who just forwarded the things on to some unknown black hole in HR.

When you ask for something, ASK.

1. Be direct. If you're the least bit vague, others may not know what you want. Tell them. "I would be so grateful if you would introduce me to David Craig in your IT department and let him know that I would be a great hire. Could you set up a meeting with him because I really need to see him in the next two weeks?" Leave the person an out. "I understand if you can't do this for me, but I am asking because I know you have really made a mark there and it would make such a difference." All of that is so much better than saying, "Can you forward my résumé to David Craig?" The résumé will get forwarded, maybe with a line of explanation, and quite probably will come and go without notice.

2. Do not look or sound desperate—even if you are. There is something sadly toxic about desperation.

3. Pay back the people who help you by doing something nice for them *and* by paying it forward. How do you help somebody who does not need your help? You say

this: "I will pay you back by helping the next person. And the next."

4. Frame the request right. Don't say, "I know you're busy, but would you . . ." Say, "You are such a force there and it would make a huge difference for me." It shows that you acknowledge the person's expertise and position.

5. Don't take advantage. If your contact is a professional who normally gets paid for what you are asking, pay them or arrange a trade. If they offer to do it free, great. I cannot tell you how often strangers ask me for free coaching, editing, writing, and advice. I am someone who likes to help others and will usually do a quick consult. But business is business.

6. If you are asking for a letter of reference from someone you know, say specifically why you want it from them. Show that you admire or respect the person and how the reference will help. Let them know what it needs to say.

7. If you get a no, don't become a pest by asking again. Sometimes there may be an occasion to quietly re-ask, but that is rare. It's usually best to move on and find a different person who will say yes.

8. Say thank you. Write a note. Give a gift. Do something.

9. It's a lot easier to ask for favors if you are known for doing favors. So be good. Help other people out.

A few years ago, a friend of mine needed a job *immediately.* She'd depleted much of her savings because her company went out of business and her foray into real estate was not working. She desperately needed help. When I heard how dire it was, I sent ten emails to highly placed people in my network with the subject line "PERSONAL FAVOR."

I shared the friend's story and how she was someone I greatly loved and respected. I wrote: "She is now looking for work and needs something as soon as possible because it has been too long without the regular paycheck and benefits. I am writing this because, more than her competence, this is someone who is one of the best human beings I have ever met. She is a team player who does the best possible job with zero drama. She was revered and adored. So she is a great hire, but she needs someone who knows someone to get this thing moving. Can you help? Do you know of anything or anyone who can help her? Do you have any job-hunting tips as far as strategies or places to apply? I am attaching her résumé."

I had never sent an email like that. I spent my clout to get some action, and let me tell you something, my network jumped on it. My friend happened into a perfectly timed job on her own, but I know my gang would have gotten her something because they were all over it. I learned something watching them jump.

Call in the chit. Put your clout on the line. I'd mentioned her to people before, but I hadn't asked for help so specifically as a favor to me. When I did, I learned the real power of networking.

When you ask for help, ASK.

15

Coming Back from a Gap

At thirty-two, Brad Taylor did the math and figured out that it wouldn't take much for him and his girlfriend to quit their IT jobs, buy a sailboat, and see the world. Two years in, the girlfriend left the boat, but he kept going and, for five years total, lived the life of most of our dreams. He went *everywhere:* South America, Australia, New Zealand, Tahiti, the Philippines—and even Africa.

"I saw a lot, had a lot of fun, but the point came where I was forcing it to keep living like that," he said. "I'd meet people, then have to move on. I had no money. I was lonely. It wasn't the exciting adventure that it was when I'd started. Everyone back home would have given anything to do what I was doing, but I wanted to go back to California and get to work."

He understood the challenge because his skills were out of date and most of his tech certifications were useless. When he plugged into his old professional network, everyone was excited to hear about his adventures, "But nobody was recommending me for any jobs because, basically, I was unhireable. That became evident pretty quickly, so I had to get a job waiting tables, borrowed money from my dad, and got the certifications I needed to get myself hired. I took so many classes and, finally, I had a résumé that said I was qualified and much more interesting than everybody else *because* I'd taken that time off. The day finally came when people started referring me for jobs."

It took two years of reeducating himself, but he finally got a good job in a university IT department and was back on track.

"If I had it to do all over again, I would do it, but I would keep doing coursework the whole time to stay current and show I was still committed to my profession," he said.

If you are thinking of taking a time-out, plan so you are thinking about reentry from the beginning, even if you aren't planning to reenter. Load yourself up with classes and experiences that will make you hirable.

And stay in constant contact with your network, because you are going to need it.

There Are Gaps and Then There Are GAPS

If you miss a year, a comeback is usually pretty easy.

Your skills are still up to date (almost). You can take an online class or two, check back in with your network, and start applying for jobs right away.

If you have taken the year to live an adventure, think about what you learned and how you can use that story to show you are an excellent candidate.

If you have taken the year to care for a loved one, that's nothing to apologize for.

And if you stayed at home with your baby? Good for you.

A year off is not a career killer.

If it was a forced time-out because of a layoff or firing, it's a little trickier because you don't want to make it look as if you have been endlessly applying for jobs, getting nowhere, and are now desperate. Frame it that you are being selective. Also, if you can show you used your time to take classes and get more skills, it looks as if you have deliberately used some of your time to upskill.

Where it gets more difficult is when you've been out of the workplace for an extended period of time. Often, your references have moved along, and some of your previous employers may have gone out of business.

I talked to one woman recently whose references and former bosses, after almost two decades, forgot who she even was. Ouch.

There are so many variables in this circumstance. How old were you when you started your gap? How much career experience did you have when you left? What kinds of jobs are you looking for? How good is your network?

Are you current?

"We tell people that every year you stay out of the workforce, you lose 10 percent of your relevance, your skill set," said career expert J. T. O'Donnell, CEO of Work It Daily, an online coaching site with monthly memberships that guide you through the job hunt process affordably. "When you're out a year, it's not so bad. Five years, six years out like most moms do when the kid goes to first grade? You are essentially back to square one. So applying online doesn't work for you unless you are applying for entry-level jobs."

Now you see why this gets trickier. The longer you have stayed out without upskilling, the harder it is to reenter the workplace. You have to look at who you are competing against. If a young graduate has current knowledge and you are just offering old experience, you've got a problem.

If your goal is to get a good job with a solid paycheck that meets or exceeds what you earned in the past, you've got to make a case for why you are worth the money. If your skills are old, it doesn't matter how much experience you *had*. It doesn't matter how good you *were*. What matters is what you can deliver on day one, and it has to be up to date.

If you are not up to date, then study everything about up-skilling, discovering trends, innovating, and plotting your course that is outlined in this book. You will get there.

O'Donnell urges people in these situations to have an "interview bucket list" where they home in on ten to twenty companies they'd like to work for, then build a network around those companies. First, connect with your own network and ask for personal contacts at those companies so you can set up informational interviews. In those interviews, you say, "I'd like to understand what you think it would take to earn a job here someday, because I am ramping back up."

"People love doing that to help moms and ex-military," O'Donnell said. "When you go in there, there is no expectation you're going to get hired, so you can make a friend and find out what it takes. The other person goes back to the office and thinks, 'She could totally do that job.' You've got your in, so when that company has a job posting, you can reach out to your connection and say, 'I saw this posting, do you think I might qualify? Could you put me in touch with the hiring manager?'"

You'll see her strategy for using LinkedIn to build the network around an interview bucket list in the full interview with O'Donnell in the chapter, "Get Yourself Hired, Part II."

Whether you have a long gap for being a parent or any other reason, there is a quick way to start getting current experience that will put you back on the path to relevance and viability.

Staffing agencies.

If you take a temporary job or temp-to-hire, you are gaining current experience, current job references, and expanding your network. The company pays the agency for the service, not you, and the agency finds a fit for your skills. They will often know of openings that aren't widely advertised. Some agencies focus on a specific industry.

The best thing they do is get you back in the game.

It may not be the easy reentry you want, but this process requires one step at a time and confidence that you are going to win in the end.

The people who lose are the ones who give up.

Just make up your mind and keep moving forward.

Life Choices and Career Gaps

I was raised by a brilliant career woman who chose to stay at home after she had children. I never judge stay-at-home parents because I was so glad I had one.

This topic is where I trip up as a career counselor. I'm someone whose work means so much to me. But it does not mean everything.

Saying so does not mean I am not committed or dedicated. It just means that I saw my mom have a stroke and become paralyzed at age sixty-six, and I know we can't put off living for later. Some people say work-life balance is impossible. I think it is possible if we know our priorities and honor them.

That is why I always cheer anybody who goes "over the wall" and takes a time-out to do something that will give their life more excitement or deeper meaning and joy.

The problem is, many people don't share that perspective. They tell themselves they can't do it, they have to play by the old rules. Or they are workaholics or type As who don't understand why others are not as obsessed or committed as they are.

Be committed to the big picture of your life.

But remember: you always have an absolute responsibility to protect your career viability because the day may come when you need to go back.

My mom taught me to always have a way to make my own money, and to have a profession that I could fall back on. She also made sure I had twenty dollars in my purse when I'd go on dates so I could get home if something went wrong. It is the same principle. You need to protect your fallback plan.

It is more complicated today because there are few professions you can walk away from for more than a year or two without losing your viability.

Even if you think you will never, ever go back, life happens. You also need to have a way to make your own money and something to do if things blow up.

So, if you are on a time-out, continue to learn, upskill, and network.

And if you are coming back after taking a time-out, there is a way back in. But you won't make it without making yourself relevant.

Stay-at-Home Moms and Dads Trying to Come Back

You should not have to apologize for doing the right thing for you, so don't. What is wrong with staying home to care for your children? NOTHING. But understand what you are up against and then be realistic about what it will take to get a great job after your extended absence.

Census data shows that roughly one in five moms and dads are full-time parents, with 25 percent of all moms and 7 percent of all dads staying home as primary caregivers. If you want to stay home with your children, you should be able to do that without judgment.

Unfortunately, the longer your time-out lasts, the more judgment you experience when you want to go back to work.

I was really impressed by what biologist turned stay-at-home mom Tania Lorena Rivera wrote about how she thinks society perceives those who make the choice to stay home. When she is in a social situation and asked what she does for a living, she notes, "I am perceived to be dependent, vulnerable, without ambition, weak, but most of all, in settings such as these, uninteresting. Not capable of entertaining an intelligent conversation that won't involve diapers and feeding schedules. A bad look for a modern woman . . . I know I am more than what these people make me out to be. I am my husband's confidante, ally, and friend. My children's protector and security blanket . . . I am the pillar on which they stand, and the glue holding this household together . . ."

Now take that bias and imagine what you are up against when you want to get back to work.

What creates that kind of attitude? I think many people are so type A that they look down on anyone who is not married to their career. And many more wish they either had the guts or resources to be able to take that time-out with their own children.

You are definitely traipsing through a high-judgment zone and I thought hard before including those statistics about reentry earlier in this book, but you've got to know what you are up against if you are going to fight a winning battle and come back.

Take a deep breath.

You have NOTHING to apologize for.

Medical or Mental Health Time-Outs

It's also a challenge coming back after a medical or mental health time-out.

The Family and Medical Leave Act allows twelve weeks of unpaid, protected leave for certain employees in certain companies. Many medical leaves stretch beyond that, and if you are taking one, you need to prepare for reentry.

First, if there is any possibility that you are going back to your previous employer, even a 1 percent chance, stay on the radar, let them know you are still around, touch base, send articles they might be interested in, whatever. It makes it so much easier to walk back in the door. And even if you think that old employer was a big part of your problem, you may need references. Just stay on good terms and in touch. You can only gain from that.

Looking for a job after this kind of a gap is challenging. First, if it is a medical leave, you have to convince new employers you are healthy. Smaller employers may fear your history will hike up their group insurance rates. Understand that.

If you took a mental health leave, and if you are open about it, you will have to deal with so much unjust stigma and judgment.

I've had several coaching clients fight for comebacks after mental health leaves, and, if they get an interview, they are always asked what happened. If they hesitate at all, if they seem uncomfortable with the question, the hiring manager notices. They aren't going to say it, but there is often an assumption that anyone who has mental health issues is weak or unstable. It is illegal for employers to discriminate against people with mental health issues under the Americans with Disabilities Act, but let's be real. They can use a million other excuses for not hiring you if they think you may have mental health issues. They may worry that you will need to take another leave or that you won't get along with others. This is an unfair judgment and an illegal bias, but it is reality.

The good thing is that employers can't access your mental health records any more than they can your medical records. They can't get information from your insurance company. All of that is private. You are not legally required to divulge the story.

The question is, How much do you say? How much do you keep to yourself?

I am all for being direct and brief. "I had a medical issue and thank goodness it is behind me now. It was a hard call to take the two-year leave, but I had no choice. I am better now and ready to go to work."

I like this approach whether your gap was caused by mental illness or cancer. Employers also are squeamish about hiring people with significant illnesses, worrying they'll have to pay more for insurance or that the person isn't fully recovered. You need to practice what you are going to say and present yourself as healthy, confident, and ready.

Be honest about it, but DO NOT OVERSHARE. Once you have said what you need to say, change the subject to your qualifications and how eager you are to get back to work. You are not required to disclose what the medical issue was, but there will be some employers who still have trouble letting it go.

Caring for a Loved One

There are so many things we should never have to explain, but we still have to do it. You should never have to explain or apologize for a career gap for caring for a loved one, but it is one of those life interruptions that costs companies a ton of money. More than one in six working Americans are devoting more than fifteen hours a week to caregiving right now, according to a recent Gallup-Healthways poll, and that number will increase considerably during this year of national and global pandemic. Fifteen percent of them will take a leave of absence for caregiving responsibilities, and 6 percent will stop working entirely. Caregivers who are employed report major issues with absenteeism, arriving late, leaving early—it's a mess. The study said 24 percent of caregivers reported that caregiving negatively impacted their work performance and cost the U.S. economy more than $25 billion in lost productivity per year.

So you can see why it can make some employers uncomfortable.

Do bosses want to be heartless? Most probably don't want to be so intentionally, but gee, I've got to go back to the day when my mother was having another surgery after suffering a stroke that permanently paralyzed her.

I was working as a reporter in Colorado, but my family lived in Florida. I'd been in Florida for a week and knew I needed another week. I had banked fifteen days of comp time by working over the holidays, and the company was delighted to let me work Christmas, Thanksgiving, and all the holidays, but guess what happened when I tried to cash them in to be there to care for my mom?

"I'm going to need to be here at least another week," I told my boss. "I have the time banked up."

"I am sorry your mom is having problems," my boss said, "but you need to get back here."

I remember getting very, very hot as I stood there, thunderstruck. Was it anger? Or was it hurt, because I'd worked so hard for him and he was being so thoughtless? I didn't think about my options, because there was only one.

"I will be staying here in Florida," I said. "I've got to go." Then, I hung up. I checked in a few days later and he actually apologized for his insensitivity, telling me a coworker berated him for it.

Our work needs to get done, which is why we are hired. But when there is an emergency and someone you love is in peril, you suddenly realize how secondary work is. I have seen people leave their loved ones to satisfy demanding bosses, but I believe family comes first, no matter what.

There will be times when your loved ones need you, and

caring for those needs may jeopardize your career. You have to make a choice. When I had that confrontation, there was no choice. I was staying longer. My dad and brother were heroic caregivers since I was so far away, but it wasn't long before I moved back to Florida so I could be there for my mom.

Being there was my life's honor. I would be so ashamed if I'd rushed back to write just another news story on just another day. So, if you have faced this decision and taken time to do what mattered to your soul, do not apologize. You weren't lounging on the beach. You were being a loving, caring human being. Bravo.

But when the time comes to go back to work or find new employment, you have to make it clear you won't need to take another time-out to provide care. You can say, "I needed to be there, and I am so glad I was. Now I am free to go back to work and won't need another leave."

You just need to convey that you have taken care of your caregiving obligations, that you will be a reliable hire, and that you don't plan on taking another leave anytime soon.

Relocation Trauma

Karen Davis was five years out of law school and right on track to become a partner in the law firm where she worked. Her husband got a great job cross-country and Davis couldn't get hired after she moved.

She stopped me after I gave a keynote on relevance.

"I don't get it," she said. "I graduated from a great school, had a great job and was very successful," she wrote. "I am so frustrated. This town is so cliquey."

I told her, "Start volunteering. Get on some boards of nonprofits. Nobody is going to turn away free legal advice. It'll show you are active and helping, and you will be instantly connected with in-fluential people who can help you meet the people you need to know."

She volunteered for the local hospice, the battered women's shelter, and the Humane Society.

About four months later, she wrote back: "I've had two job interviews and one more coming. I've already gotten an offer, but the job wasn't what I am looking for. I know it's all because of the volunteer work. I'm meeting the right people. I know the right job is coming. Plus, I've found I love volunteering."

Great lesson. Volunteering for nonprofits is a great way to feel good about yourself, build skills, *and* get connected to people who can dramatically improve your local professional network. They'll see you as a peer when you are volunteering and, when you make it clear what you want, people will help you. It grows your professional network, but just as important, it grows your personal network when you are new in town. You just need the right people to know how fabulous you are.

Coming Back, Post-Gap

Rita Stepp lost her job as part of a workforce reduction, but she'd been there long enough to retire. The first thing she did was take a break.

"I took the first four months to 'rest'; be quiet, reflect, and mourn the loss," she said. "I investigated a cost-effective gym, signed with a personal trainer, and began a rigorous exercise program." She joined her condo board, started learning how to do minor repairs to the properties, and took a few classes. Now she is on the hunt for a job.

"I absolutely embrace the truth that randomly applying for job postings rarely works," she said. "I am taking the neces-sary time to be strategic in my approach to the job hunt, which includes deciding what I want to do next, understand who I am as a professional, have social presence, understand and develop my 'niche.' And, NETWORK, NETWORK, NEWORK!"

I really like her positive attitude. Despite the difficulties, she is making many friends in the process, something she considers a real bonus.

Her head is definitely in the game.

"Take a defined time to REST; R = Reflect, E = Enjoy family/ friends, S = Spend time taking inventory of who you are and what you want, T = remember to give Thanks because you are more than your last position," she said. "Then, be strategic in your job search: find an organization that truly helps job seekers, do the necessary steps, network, have a social presence, find the job, and never stop looking and growing!"

Andrea Bjorkman took a time-out after leaving her last job a year and a half ago. She either needed to accept the severance package or another job that likely would have been a demotion.

"I took almost nine months off to spend time with my family—both of my parents are eighty-seven and are dealing with health issues—and friends," she said. "I got my Pilates mat certification, really took up running and ran my first half-marathon, got even more involved in my charity work, did some leadership coaching, took many online classes to learn new skills, and worked on my personal growth."

Now that she's trying to find work, she's having trouble.

"It's been very interesting to be on this side of job hunting," she said. "It has been eighteen years since I looked for a job. I did just turn sixty and despite all I do to hide my age, I do wonder if that is hurting me."

So she doesn't advertise her age, and her résumé includes only fifteen years of experience but does not list the year she got her bachelor's degree. She does say she earned her MBA in 2007.

She's had more than thirty phone interviews, which is amazing.

"There have been a few times where I shared other experiences I've had that are relevant to the job I'm interviewing for that are not on my résumé. Then I'm asked why I didn't include them!"

She's done four video interviews and, twice, men who were older than she were doing the interviews.

"They asked how much longer I wanted to work. Both of them prefaced their questions with something like, 'HR will be mad at me for this,' but that sure didn't stop them."

I liked how she processed it all: "I strongly believe the reasons I was given for not getting an offer were valid, but I can't believe my age didn't help them feel better about their decision," she said.

One step closer to the next opportunity.

Heather Nivver was facing special challenges when trying to get another job. When we connected, she had been out of work nine months after her entire department was dissolved. She has a preschooler and used to work at home as an editor and writer in a full-time remote position.

"A similar situation has been hard to find," she said. "With a three-and-a-half-year-old, I have to find a job that can be done remotely or pays enough to make paying for childcare worthwhile," she said. That was proving to be a challenge.

She was sending out résumés and researching opportunities every week. She signed up for J. T. O'Donnell's Work It Daily program for advice and took online courses in copywriting and social media marketing.

But it's been really hard.

"It's my purgatory," she said. "I hate selling myself to others and playing the job-search game. I hoped to find something right away, even if it wasn't my dream job, but that obviously hasn't worked out. I was laid off once before and took a warehouse job to get the bills paid. I hated it. Work It Daily has helped a lot, though! I've had a few interviews and bites . . . and have some possibilities on the horizon."

Her unemployment benefits have ended, and since her husband is self-employed and winter is his slow time, they are forced to be creative to get their bills paid.

"It's stressful," she said.

Kimberly Burke is just now gearing up after a seventeen-year time-out to raise her daughter. She's getting ready to start applying for jobs.

"It's very overwhelming!" she said. "So much has changed since I had to look for a full-time job. I have spent six to eight weeks just trying to catch up on how to rewrite my résumé, set up a LinkedIn account, study how to apply and prepare for interviews," she said.

She lists the gap on her résumé as "caregiver" and says, "I have not applied for any jobs yet but I assume that it will have an impact in my search because of how long the gap is."

Her gap's biggest impact has been "On my confidence on getting back into the workforce," she said. "The longer I stayed out, the harder it got to want to get back in because I did not see my value as a stay-at-home mom. Looking back, I recognize I could have been doing more to make the transition back into the workforce easier for me, such as writing my résumé, networking, training and continuing to work part-time."

There is so much you can do to grow your value while you are searching for a job. So take a minute and strategize:

1. **Volunteer.** Is there a volunteer opportunity that will give you exposure to some of the players who can get you hired elsewhere? What volunteer experience

will expand or showcase your skill set? And what will make you feel good?

2. **Get on a board.** Is there a nonprofit that needs your talent and brilliance? What a great way to showcase your skills and your presence—and usually in a way that makes you feel great for contributing.

3. **Deep dive into social media.** This is not just about posting birthday photos on Facebook. It is time to learn what you need to know about maximizing your presence on LinkedIn, Instagram, Facebook, and Twitter. You can take a course and then come up with a "content schedule" that will give you a business plan for how you will use social media to promote yourself and get the opportunities you want and need.

4. **Take courses!** Much more on this throughout the book, but this is the time to take advantage of the multitude of excellent online courses that will make you current, relevant, and prime for hiring.

5. **Have fun.** You'll have enough busywork once your are on to bigger and better things professionally. Don't forget to fill your downtime with joy and fun.

16

Coming Back from a National Crisis

The economy has collapsed on me three times in the last twenty years. There was 9/11, the Great Recession of 2008, and now there is the COVID-19 pandemic.

The virus crisis will, I hope, be a memory by the time you read this. But, eventually, something else will happen; it will be big, people will face great fear and hardship, and you will wonder what you need to do to make it to the other side.

Always remember: your greatest opportunity to succeed occurs in moments when everybody else is giving up.

Each of those national emergencies resulted in massive layoffs and a gutted economy. The bad news was endless. People froze with fear and worry. Many panicked.

Some seized the moment.

There will be times when you will be forced by circumstance to regroup and, perhaps, start over. Whether the crisis is a pandemic, terrorist attack, hurricane, flood, wildfire, an economic collapse, or something personal, it is on you to get it together and find your strongest self as quickly as possible. We face a crisis, recover, and then another one is waiting.

That can depress you or challenge you.

At the moment, I could feel really rotten about what has

happened to my business. All my speaking events have been canceled because conferences are large events, and we can't gather in large groups. Poor me. I could become depressed because of what has happened to my investment portfolio.

But NO.

It is likely the convention industry will be in the crapper for at least a year, probably two. So I'll reinvent. My superpower is information. I'm good at content. I'm good at delivery. I have set up a production studio in my home and I'm putting out courses on all the lessons in this book and my others. The one thing I know is this: right here in this shared moment of helplessness, I will find my moment to rise up, take charge, and shine.

And do you know what? I'm going to win. I've made up my mind, a decision that has eliminated almost all of my stress. I am so certain I will succeed that I am just enjoying the adventure.

Accept, cope, and adapt.

Because of what I learned during 9/11 and the Great Recession, I know that I am not going to play the victim. I will rise up. I am standing on home plate with the bases loaded. I'm going to study what I am up against, focus, and swing HARD because I want to win.

My self-talk is 100 percent positive. Is yours?

It is easy to find excuses about why things will be difficult, why we're going to have trouble, why anyone over fifty is going to struggle ten times harder. But why pollute our brains with any of that? Even if some of those things are true, they are not 100 percent true. Instead of wallowing in all the uncertainty and negativity, start envisioning your opportunity on the other side of the crisis.

When my first book came out, my national tour was canceled because my publisher assumed all media coverage would go to 9/11 and the subsequent anthrax threat. Being a former media person, I knew the attention span of Americans was short. At some point, they were going to be *hungry* for something positive. They would want all the hope and inspiration that my book *Hard Won Wisdom* shared.

My editor stood solidly behind me, but my publisher gave up. The book was out there on the shelves. It *had* to sell within the first three months, or it would be sent back to make room for the next round of books coming out. I had to make it sell right then in that moment of crisis.

Teresa Searcy, the marketing manager in my area from Borders bookstore (remember them?), called me and said, "We just got the weirdest email from your publisher. It says, 'Understandably, the author has decided not to tour at this time for safety concerns.' So you can't drive from North Tampa to South Tampa?"

"Of course I can," I said. "They've given up on it."

"Well," Teresa said. "Why are *you* giving up? I know every Borders person you need to know in the country. Get out there."

I'd been a starving author for the three years before my book's release and was almost broke. I'd bet everything on it. Her encouragement and support in that moment changed my life forever. She made me rise up and take ownership of my future.

I pulled out a legal pad and wrote down the cities all over the country where I had friends and relatives who would let me bunk with them. I used my last money to rent a Ford Escort and got in the car to promote *Hard Won Wisdom* for three weeks.

The window was wide open to succeed because everyone else had given up.

No authors were touring, so I received a ton of media coverage everywhere I went. I went to my former stomping grounds of Denver for the book signing I'd always dreamed of at my favorite bookstore, the Tattered Cover. About a hundred of my old friends showed up. They had a contest to prove who loved me the most by the quantity of books they bought. I will never forget my friend Miriam Reed buying twenty-five copies of *Hard Won Wisdom* at $24.95 each.

They turned me into a bestselling author.

Remember: during tough times, your friends and family will get you there.

And, again, the window is wide open to succeed in moments when everyone else is giving up.

I was driving my rented Ford Escort from Chicago to St. Louis through a snowstorm. The phone rang, and the publicist for my book said, "The TV station called us and canceled your appearance because they are doing a whole show on anthrax tomorrow."

I was almost to St. Louis, where I was staying with my friend Dianne Williams, a former TV newsperson. Without that TV interview, nobody would know about my book signing.

But when the door slams shut, you have to kick it back open or find a window.

"I was just thinking," I said to Dianne, "that the TV station knows they canceled the interview. The publicist knows they canceled the interview. But the TV station does not know that the publicist reached me to tell me they canceled the interview."

"And?"

"What if I just showed up?"

"Well, I don't know how they'd squeeze you in, but how could it hurt?"

I got up early, put on my suit, and drove to Channel 5 in downtown St. Louis. I signed in and sat amongst the "real" guests who were waiting to be called back for the show. The director came out and looked down the list of guests, and I noted his surprise when he saw my name on the list. He motioned for me to come over to him.

"I'm really sorry, but we had to cancel your appearance," he said. "We called your publicist yesterday. This show is all about anthrax."

"*What?*" I said, acting utterly shocked. "*I drove all the way here from Chicago, just for this.*"

"You did?" he asked. He was calculating something in his head. "Is there any way you could come back tomorrow?"

"Well," I said. "I guess so."

OMG, it worked. Then it got even better.

"The problem is, I don't have a writer for your segment," he said.

"I'm a writer," I said. "I'd be happy to write it."

Now, letting a guest write their own segment? That is NOT journalistically allowable, and I have no idea why he allowed it. But, on that particular day, he brought me back to the newsroom, and I wrote the best interview segment anyone would ever do with me: all kinds of slow-pitch, easy questions that showcased my book and personality.

When I came back the next day for my appearance, they gave me a whole three minutes of airtime—which is a lot, because most segments are one and a half to two minutes. They put up a big slide about my book signing at Borders that night, and my signing was *packed*. It was one of the biggest signings I ever had at a bookstore.

A woman came up to me after I spoke and said, "I run the Working Women's Survival Show in St. Louis and Omaha, and you need to be one of my keynote speakers."

My life changed forever, right then. My speaking career was

born. All because, in a time when everyone else had given up, I put on my suit and risked looking like a complete fool by showing up at that television station.

When others are focused on their struggles, step aside for a minute. Look around. What can you do? There is *always* something.

I kept writing letters to Oprah Winfrey during that time. Thousands of authors wanted their books on *Oprah,* and it was nearly impossible to pull off. I wrote twenty-nine letters suggesting potential shows.

"You are obsessing," said my agent, Caroline Carney.

"Caroline, twenty-nine is not obsessing," I said. "Thirty is obsessing."

We laughed.

One of the twenty-nine worked. She held up my book and told the world it was "very inspiring," and then things really started rolling for me. I am absolutely convinced it is because so many authors, publicists, and publishers stayed off the road when everything seemed to stop during the 9/11 attacks.

And yet success was right there waiting for them.

I broke through, and that cleared the way for me to really soar as an author and speaker.

To be honest, my second book was better than my first. Oprah didn't take it. I am sure it's because thousands of authors were sending inquiries again. The window was wide open after 9/11, but others didn't see it.

That taught me such a lesson about rising up when others are hunkering down. There is an opening. There is an opportunity. What are you going to do to seize it?

When the Great Recession hit, I knew the speaking business was likely to take a hit. If companies were laying off tens of thousands of employees, they were going to be mighty careful bringing in outside speakers and hosting expensive conferences and events. But I told myself, "Even if the industry gets cut in half, that leaves half of the business for me."

So I sat down at my keyboard and started writing as fast as I could. I wrote the book *Finding the Up in the Downturn.* My team of editors and designers worked in hyperdrive. In six weeks, the book was written, edited, designed, produced, and in print, with my picture branded on the cover. That was important because, yes, it was a book about dealing with adversity in a time of crisis, but more than that, it was my press kit to get me speaking at the companies that were trying to teach their people exactly that. That book sold thousands of copies, and it led to so many speaking engagements, where companies would buy the book for every person in the audience. In a year when others struggled in my industry, my business skyrocketed.

All of that opportunity came because I quickly figured out how to pivot.

Worst-Case Scenario

Time holds the answers we don't always see. Things do tend to work out in some way. They do.

I always say to myself, "What's the worst thing that can happen?" Well, I could die. I believe in life after death, which would be kind of cool. But if there is no life after death, I'll be dead, so it won't matter. I don't fear death.

That doesn't mean I don't try to protect myself, and as I write this I am very serious about that while I am practicing social distancing. I do *not* want the virus, but I just have faith that everything will work out okay.

By the time you read this, my hope is that these struggles will be really old news and the economy will be cranking once again. But the lessons of the pandemic are truly the same as from the Great Recession and 9/11.

Every so often, everything unravels. Your ability to rebound depends entirely on your ability (and willingness) to accept, cope, and adapt.

Suck It Up

Even those who fail to accept, cope, and adapt quickly are forced to adapt at some point. You have two options in crisis:

1. Surrender to panic, stress, fear, anxiety, and worry.
2. Buck the fuck up.

Ask yourself: Who is going to prevail in a crisis? The one who panics or freezes up, or the person who bucks up, deals with it, and carries on?

Which person do you choose to be? It *is* a choice. The faster you get it together, the faster you get on with life.

Have faith that it will work out in the end.

When I turned forty, I looked back on my life and realized something about every crisis I had ever faced: they all ended. So remember that when life gets especially tough: every shit storm ends.

Choosing to Win

It might appear unseemly to focus on winning at a time when people are sick, dying, and in financial ruin. But what is your other choice? To curl up in a fetal position, glued to cable news and waiting for the end of days? Life is going to go on. Every crisis ends. *Not* thinking about how you are going to prevail on the other side of it is foolish.

Granted, if your house is the one that loses its roof in a hurricane, you have to deal with that rather than plot out career strategies. But unless you are a direct victim, get it together and get on with things. Figure out the steps you need to take. Write down the people you need to call. Then do the steps and call the people!

If you are not a direct victim or your situation is not life-threatening, you have to buck up and start brainstorming what you need to do to maintain your level of success. If you are not sick and your house is still standing, you need to decide where your opening is.

Your business, job, or finances may have suffered greatly, and you can complain, worry, and stress yourself all you want, but at some point you have to dig your way out of it. Don't wait.

Are you going to wait until things get "back to normal," then figure it out? The people who act quickly reap the rewards. How are you going to emerge from the crisis as a go-to player at work? How are you going to be positioned to be the first hired?

The pandemic has pushed people to the brink, but anyone stuck at home and who is not sick has a ton of time to get in shape and take classes that will upskill them and prepare them to rise above coworkers or other job applicants. This book hits hard on your need to upskill, and you can do it instantly—for free or minimal cost—at many online learning sites (my favorites are edx.org and coursera.org).

And yet most people are still sitting at home wondering what the hell happened and what is going to happen next.

What a waste of time!

No News Is Good News

If you want things to look bleak, watch the news. If you want things to look hopeless, keep watching the news.

But if you want to maintain control over your sanity, start tuning it out.

Yes, you are being encouraged to institute a partial-news

blackout in tough times by someone who lived, breathed, and loved her first career as a journalist.

In times of national crisis, you have to take charge of your news intake or it will take charge of you.

Of course you need to know what is going on.

But when all the news is bad, it makes you feel bad. Decide how much you need to read or watch in order to be informed, but not consumed by it. You don't need every little detail and you don't need to know what twenty pontificators have to say about the latest development. You can check it once a day, once every two or three days, and maybe once a week if you can discipline yourself. If something important happens that you absolutely must know, you'll know it—either because someone will tell you about it or you'll see it on social media. But the more you watch, the more the problem grows inside of your brain.

The constant coverage distorts reality. When you see headlines warning that the unemployment rate may hit 16 percent—yikes! How does that make you feel about your chances of applying for and getting a job?

What does your brain do when you constantly read about people dying, going broke, unable to afford food, being laid off en masse? It creates the worst possible reality for you—one that doesn't even exist.

If you tune it out (or at least way down), your brain can control its own perspective. Minimizing exposure helps you process these circumstances to your best advantage.

Power Networking in Crisis

Technology makes it so easy to connect with others in a meaningful way during a crisis. That's why it is so easy to collaborate from home from our computers and phones. As I mentioned earlier, the lockdown wasn't a roadblock to networking. It was an open invitation to get serious about it! I sent texts to so many people in my network and we all had endless time to catch up and deepen our friendships. I knew nobody was doing anything and with a Zoom invite, we were suddenly all together, in living color, having our wine, catching up, and enjoying a great moment of friendship.

Look at the people you know and start making contact with everybody. Brainstorm together. You support them; they support you. Whether you are stuck at home or things are more normal, you can always Zoom them. FaceTime them. Do whatever you can to keep the friendship going strong.

Let them know what you are struggling with and ASK FOR HELP.

Take Charge of Your Thoughts

I can't say this enough: you are in charge of your brain. It believes what you tell it. So if you tell it that you are going to suffer, you will suffer. If you expect trouble, you'll find trouble. If you tell yourself you're going to be unemployed forever or you will be old, sick, broke, and alone, guess what? Your brain is more than happy to help you manifest that gloomy outlook.

That is why it is especially important that you monitor your thoughts and overpower the negative during a crisis you can't control.

Affirmations will help you program your brain for the ideas you might have trouble with. Some examples for dealing with adversity in times of crisis are:

- I am safe, healthy, and strong.
- I easily let go of worry over things I can't control.

- I am actively strategizing ways to seize the moment and be successful.
- Success is coming my way.
- I know everything will work out.
- I love my life.
- I am open, creative, and constantly coming up with great ideas that will make me more successful.
- I will win.

Repeat, repeat, repeat. Twenty times a day, fifty times a day—until you realize your brain has become positive and is helping you win despite (or even because of) a national crisis.

Consider the company you are keeping. If you surround yourself with incessant worriers or complainers, they will pollute your positive brain space. Keep away from negative people.

Companies Are Crying Out for Good Leaders

When companies are in crisis, they need leadership and contribution. What a great time to stand up and lead. Your greatest contribution can come when you see a problem and know how to fix it. The greatest way to expand authority is to volunteer to solve an unmet need.

Basically, your stepping up and fixing something means your boss doesn't have to do it. So keep your eyes open for any opportunity to contribute more.

Do you see ways to do something differently that will save money or time? Do you know of ways to attract more business or generate more revenue? Are there other problems you can solve? Speak up. Step up. Do it.

Even if you don't have an idea, you do have the ability to make it clear that you want to be a go-to contributor during the crisis and are ready to volunteer to do more. This makes you stand out. If you need to remind leadership of your special skills and abilities, do it.

Be seen as part of the solution—not the problem. This may not insulate you from a layoff, but it will certainly help.

Make it clear that you are embracing change and work harder than you have ever worked. Hyperperformance will separate you from the others, and those who deliver generally give themselves good job security.

Just overdeliver, overdeliver, overdeliver.

It's your time to shine.

Fall Down Seven Times, Get Up Eight

Don't just sit there waiting for your company to toss you out. Always be ready for anything.

Have your résumé, cover letter, and wardrobe ready for your intense networking and job search. Identify the companies where you want to look for jobs and know that, among all the many people who will be looking for jobs, you are more organized and your brain is in the game.

You'll need all of the skills described in this book, but if you are searching in a time when everyone is searching, you will also need a sense of calm and a sense of humor. It's going to be a tough, wild ride, but the person who will be victorious will know with certainty that they will prevail.

I know it is hard to stay calm when your financial situation is precarious or your finances are in ruin. It's difficult to have a sense of humor when you try, try, try and get rejected at every turn. But you know that your attitude drives happiness and success. If you mentally make the decision to stay in the game, stay in it. Be good to yourself. Know that "this too shall pass." If you know it, it will be your truth.

Go There

During tough times, I have seen numerous friends teetering on bankruptcy. Some declared; others didn't. I know many people who gave up or lost their homes to foreclosure or short sales. I have had friends wonder how they were going to survive.

I remember one good friend coming to me—desperate. Her husband had just been laid off. She'd been laid off two months earlier. They were losing their beautiful home. They were running out of savings.

What can you say to someone when all hope is lost?

"Pray," I said. Because when you lose hope, you still have faith. Faith creates hope, and hope leads you to your path.

They did lose the house but cobbled together some freelance work, and soon both had jobs. Then they bought another house. Their kids got married. There were grandchildren.

They were happy again. Life was different—not as prosperous—but it was much richer.

I don't mean to sugarcoat hardship, because there are many, many people who do not easily find their way out of such difficulties. But my point here is that when hope is lost, count on whatever spirituality you choose to help you get through the impossible. I believe that, when there are no answers, your faith is the answer.

Ride the Roller Coaster

When you buckle into a good roller coaster, you've got a few seconds of *clickity click click* and massive anticipation that things are about to go crazy. A hill! A drop! Twists and turns! Another hill! Another drop! More twists and curves!

Then it all evens out, and you coast to the end of the track.

That's what happens during a major crisis: out-of-control, fast, and with unexpected ups and downs, twists and turns.

But it always ends.

You may not have enjoyed the ride and you may be very shaken, but it ends.

So hang in there. Yes, life can throw you around and scare the hell out of you, but it's going to slow down; there will be a new normal, and life will go on.

I hope that you will come through your challenges stronger and more successful. There is opportunity out there. Remember that. The window is wide open. And when you experience those highs and lows, remember that your friends and family will get you there.

It'll be okay.

Every shit storm ends.

17

Get Yourself Hired, Part I

Back when I was a starving author who could not find a publisher for my first book, I started applying for jobs. I needed money urgently.

My local community college posted an opening for a journalism professor, and I knew it was perfect for me. I'd taught undergraduate and graduate students part-time for a dozen years. I'd worked at great newspapers and won awards for breaking news coverage, investigative reporting, and feature writing. I had four Pulitzer Prize nominations.

I should have been a shoo-in, but I never even got an interview.

Being a journalist, I knew all of the hiring records were open to the public. I submitted a public records request to see all of the applications and the list of those who were interviewed.

It turned out they only interviewed one person—the guy they hired. He had no journalism experience—zero. He'd hosted a Saturday radio show in a small town in Iowa. When I complained about this to a friend of mine who was a professor at the school, she said, "Oh, that guy has been teaching here part-time for a few years. He knows everybody. That was a done deal before it was even posted."

Every time I tell that story, someone shares a similar experience.

The point is that you can be the very best candidate yet not land the job or even an interview or a response. There is no formula for getting hired. If you don't get the job, don't process it as a rejection. It's not always about you. It may be about them, timing, your competition, personalities, who knows who, or office politics. It is often about hidden factors other than who would be the best hire.

It doesn't make sense and it won't.

All you can do is keep trying until you hit.

This chapter will give you some ideas of what to do as you search for a job. If you follow every step, your odds will be better. But I know there is so much about the hiring process that will never make sense to us.

If you are already employed, try to stay employed. You've heard this a million times before: it is always easier to get a job when you have a job. Keep your job as long as you can. It makes you more attractive as a candidate and gives you more leverage when you are negotiating.

But if you have quit, been laid off, or flat-out fired, get moving. Have a massive pity party the first day, lick your wounds the second day, then get moving. For starters:

Quickly build a grid, calendar, or task list with goals and deadlines. That way you know what you have to do every single day to move toward success. Check out this list every morning and, at the end of the day, say, "What have I done today to move myself toward my goal?" This is important because job hunting can be an infuriating, demeaning process. You may find yourself having to woo people who have one-tenth the experience you have. You may be passed over by people who aren't nearly as smart as you. The only way to keep your spirits up is to have a list of steps that will always give you something to do when you don't feel like doing anything.

Don't dawdle; get moving and keep moving. This is not the time to take a vacation! Your prospects are greatest during the first five weeks after you become unemployed, so run hard and fast.

Dive into LinkedIn, and take a course in how to get the most out of it. There are a million courses in it. Don't just feel your way around. LinkedIn advertises you to the world. It gives you access to just about everyone you could want to access. Use it to make yourself appear to be an expert in your field, which will make others want to hire you.

Google, Google, Google. You can look up examples of résumés specific to your industry. You can search for the right keywords that showcase your skills. You can study the companies you wish to target and learn so much about their leaders. You can get interview tips and strategies.

Fill out online applications, but don't count on them. The average online posting gets at least 250 responses. Jobvite's 2017 study concluded that referrals are five times more likely to get you a job than all other hiring resources. Networking is most important.

Stay busy. Plan out your day, week, and month. You have to know what you are going to do next; otherwise, you risk stalling out. You always have to have a plan for next steps so you can stay positive and maintain momentum.

Know What You Want

I interviewed a man who told me about his informational interview with the CEO of a company with more than a thousand employees. He told the CEO how smart he was and that he'd be a great hire.

"What are you looking for?" the executive asked.

"I've got a lot of experience and knowledge, and I'm very creative. What do you have that you think I'd be great at?" he asked.

The CEO said nothing for the longest time, then finally spoke.

"I need you to know what you want," he said.

The man started reciting his experience and skills, but the CEO just looked at him like he was wasting his time.

"Well, I can't help you," the CEO said. "But I have to give you some advice here: you need to figure these things out before you ask somebody for a job."

Whoa.

The meeting ended quickly, and the guy complained about how cold and dismissive the CEO was.

Seriously? Why is it on someone else to solve what you can't solve for yourself? It's not up to them to tell you what your next job should be. It's up to you to study what's out there and figure out what, where, and how you want to contribute.

I can't tell you how many times people have shared fabulous résumés that tell potential employers nothing about what they are looking for. What are hiring managers supposed to do with a vaguely targeted résumé when they are inundated with résumés from people who actually scrutinized the posting, studied the company, and *do* have goals and plans for themselves?

It is invaluable to brainstorm the possibilities with the people who best know your strengths and skills, but don't rely on your professional contacts to figure out your life. If you don't know what you want to do, start taking free online interest surveys and career tests. Go to the career guidance office at your community college. Hire a life coach. Just don't expect other people to do the work you need to do.

Leveraging Your Network

This book has an entire chapter on leveraging your network, but I want to reiterate some ideas, because your network is your greatest resource, and if you are a wuss about it, your network is useless.

Glassdoor reports that the average job posting attracts at least 250 applicants. Only 2 percent will get an interview. That's five people out of 250. You can take it personally if you want, but those odds suck.

So what can you do to get pulled out of the pile?

Leverage your network and take risks.

Who is usually the first to know when a position is coming open? Glassdoor or people in the company? People employed in the company generally know who is quitting, when there will be hiring for a restructuring, and what's coming in the new budget year long before any job is posted online. That's why so many placements are done deals before the post goes live. People are already making the case for filling from within or hiring somebody they know would be a perfect fit. Just get on the radar with the companies you want to work for so you can learn early what's coming open and who your point person is.

Give yourself one intense hour every day to connect and reconnect with people who can help or people who know the people who can help. Don't make this networking all about you. It's also about them. Connect, reconnect, find out what's going on with them, and then ask for what you need.

Be sincere, respectful, and don't come off as a shameless taker.

I received a nice wedding gift from a student in a university journalism class I taught years ago. I couldn't believe she thought so much of me to give me that lovely tray and coaster set.

But then she said this: "You are going to be so good for my career."

Oh yeah, I still remember her—three decades later. She is a great example of how *not* to network.

The trick is to ask others for help in a way that makes them want to help you because they like you. People do favors for people they like, not people who are simply using them.

I recently received this note from an acquaintance: "I never expected I would be starting over again at age 58, but here I am. I really need help from you and anyone you know who can help me to get an interview at PWC. I see that you are connected to several people in leadership there. Can you contact them and get me plugged in? I need your help and am so grateful for anything you can do for me, and of course, let me know if there is anything I can do for you."

Perfect. She told me specifically what she needed and wasn't pushy. Of course I helped her get plugged in.

Assess the people in your network to figure out how they can help you and how much you can ask of them. Then spend some time thinking about how to frame your ask. Be sincere, appreciative, and specific. Sometimes, the best thing you can get from a well-placed stranger is the name and contact information of the person doing the hiring—and that's valuable because companies usually hide that name so they aren't besieged by inquiries.

One college graduate told me she wrote every single member of the executive board of an organization I have done a lot of work for, asking for help getting a job. This young woman is fantastic, and would have been a great hire for every one of the companies those board members worked for. I knew every member of that board and saw them as true mentors, so imagine my shock when only one actually made the calls that got her hired. A few gave advice and shipped her résumé to HR with a note. But some people—people I would expect more from—didn't even answer her email.

She did get a job out of it, so her tactic was a home run. But you can't necessarily count on thorough action from your entire network. The lesson is to make sure you are making multiple asks and follow up until you get an answer.

The Letter, the Résumé

Your best possible entrée is through somebody. Just get in the door, then win them over by showing how current, with it, and excited you are.

But you still need a résumé and cover letter.

Think about the person who is going through the applications. What are they looking for? Don't just say you meet every qualification required for the job. Look up the company! What is it that you know/do that specifically will help the company? And learn how to write a fabulous disruptive cover letter, just like career expert J. T. O'Donnell explains in the next chapter.

Don't just say that you are a good fit: show it by demonstrating that you have done your homework. Not only do you know what it will take to succeed in the position, but you know what it will take to help the company at this precise moment. You should prove that you are the right person to help if the company is rebounding out of tough times, dealing with a merger or transition, or facing unprecedented growth. Show that you have a serious interest in that specific job at that specific company and that you are the right person to help them deal with change and move into the future.

The résumé you need is different than the résumé you cranked out in the past. These days, you do not want a five-page résumé with a tiny font saying how amazing you are.

Career expert O'Donnell says recruiters are given a list of what a candidate must have and you have to pass the first cut. If you highlight all of your skills, education, degrees, and certifications at the top of your résumé, it is easy for recruiters to see that you offer everything they need to deliver to their clients.

Only list ten years of jobs. Any more will date you. A killer summary sentence or two at the beginning is the best way to convey the force of your accomplishments.

I've had two big careers. Recruiters don't need to see every newspaper that I worked for, but don't you think it helps to say somewhere that, in addition to what I am doing now, I also had a successful career as an investigative reporter for some of the nation's best newspapers?

Before you choose your format, spend time searching online and develop more than one approach for companies that have different cultures. A young and energetic company is going to respond to something very different from how an old, stodgy company will. Figure out what will play best by reading online reviews posted by employees who describe their work environments. Glassdoor can be a good source for that information, as well as employee chat rooms and other places for dialogue about specific industries or companies.

Also, do not plagiarize from sample résumés and cover letters online. Simply use them for inspiration. Plagiarism is easy to detect, because the people you are competing against are looking at the same sample résumés and cover letters and may steal the same ideas and language. You won't get the job if you and another person turn in the same content. Besides, it's lazy. It lacks integrity. Don't do it.

Do let the massive information on the Internet spark your creativity to customize the best résumés and cover letters that advertise you and only you. What you find online can be a huge help—but don't make it your crutch.

Because so much of the hiring process is now automated, it's difficult to avoid the standardization that comes when you list your jobs and the dates you worked. If you leave off the dates, you will score zero for experience. And, while experience is not valued like it used to be, computers are still scoring it to rank applicants. You don't want zeros.

Definitely leave off your graduation dates for school. Those dates automatically reveal your age, the assumption being that you got your bachelor's degree when you were twenty-two to twenty-four years old. It is very common for companies to ask the year you graduated high school, which is an obvious way of figuring out precisely how old the applicants are but totally legal.

If you are older, you're older. There is nothing you can do about it. To make your age work for you, showcase yourself as an active, creative professional who is not only current on technology and trends but also a change leader.

And, again, your best way in is with the endorsement of somebody who already works there.

The Interview

You don't need me to tell you that you need to look the part when you show up for an interview. We all know that. Unfortunately, we may not have a very good idea of what the part looks like these days. If the environment is youth-oriented and laid-back, you've got to choose style over formality. You need an idea of what the place looks like and what the people who are interviewing you are likely to be wearing.

If you are unsure, just ask what the dress code is in the office. Yes. ASK. "Not sure what people are wearing there and before I put on my ball gown or tuxedo, I thought I'd ask."

Whatever you wear, wear it well. Wear it with confidence. You may feel a little wobbly trying to resurrect your confidence as you achieve your comeback, so it may be easier to just fake it. Show up as the most confident version of yourself that ever existed. Think of a day when you felt awesome and bring that version of yourself to the interview. If you project confidence in yourself, others will feel confident in you.

Do not call attention to your age or your interviewer's age. Don't make a joke about it. Don't say you have a son or daughter or grandchild that is their age.

If you are overqualified, be ready to explain why you would settle for less money or a lesser title than you've enjoyed in the past. You need to convey that you aren't looking for a placeholder job until you find something better (even if you are). What you say is, "I am passionate about working and I just want to stay in the game or to make a new beginning, if that is what you seek. This company would be perfect because . . ."

Make it clear you are tech savvy. So many people tell me they are good with technology, when they are utterly ignorant compared to a recent graduate. So tout the courses you have taken to make you current. Make it clear you know, use, and embrace many forms of social media. If you haven't been active on Twitter, LinkedIn, Instagram, and Facebook, start posting NOW, and do it every day. That way, when your interviewers check you out, they'll see that you are active. Will they spend enough time to drill down to see that you weren't posting anything three months ago? Unlikely. Just make up for it now. And google technology trends for the industry so you can talk about what's coming and make it clear you are part of the future.

Be specific about accomplishments. Saying that you have managed a ninety-person staff or a $15 million budget or have exceeded your sales goals by more than $1 million a quarter are concrete examples of your experience, value, and preparedness.

Have stories ready! Pick engaging anecdotes that show your value as a contributor, team member, and leader. Think them through so they aren't too short or too long. Know in advance what the stories are supposed to illustrate so you can show how it was either a defining moment, great lesson, huge success, or failure that led to big success. People love engaging stories, but rehearse your material in advance.

What stories are on your list? What stories show how you persevere? Win people over? Close a deal? Face obstacles? Take risks? Bring out the best in others? Rebound after failing? Start your own list, and be comfortable with your own material. Your stories will make your interview stand out.

Watch your tone. It is important to sound respectful and appreciative, not desperate, demanding, know-it-all, or insincere.

Never sound desperate. I interviewed two-time Academy Award winner Frances McDormand for my first book, and she said something I have always remembered: if she went into an audition and they could see she was desperate for a particular part, directors didn't want her. She learned to hide her desperation because desperate people make others uncomfortable. It is a tricky dance to do—especially when you really are desperate. That doesn't mean you have to pretend life is perfect, but do not look hopeless or helpless; do not break down in tears; do not vent all of your frustrations to the people you are counting on to propel you forward. They want to support a winner. So project a winner.

Also, it doesn't hurt to make it seem as if you are fielding other offers. I make my living speaking. Does a meeting planner want someone with an empty schedule or someone who other companies are trying hard to get for their own events?

It's always good to sound a little busy. You can indicate that you are being courted for positions in locations you don't necessarily want, but be careful about it. Just a slight hint that there is something going on.

Do not assume that the person who is interviewing you has read your résumé or cover letter or that the person knows any more than your name. An interview is your moment to sell yourself as a contributor and a human being.

Have answers ready. I'll list the most common interview questions because they are common for a reason. There are thousands of resources online that tell you how to answer them. But expect versions of . . .

1. Tell me about yourself.
2. What are your greatest strengths?
3. Weaknesses?
4. What makes you want to work for us?
5. Why should we bring you on board?
6. Tell me about your goals.
7. What do you want to be doing in five years?
8. Why did you leave your last job?
9. What do you bring to us that the other candidates don't?
10. Why do you want this particular job?
11. What is your greatest achievement?
12. Describe your ideal job.
13. Describe your ideal workplace.
14. What do you do for fun?
15. Do you have any questions for me?

Ask questions. This is also a great moment to connect with the interviewer and find out why they chose the company and what their experience has been. It also is an opportunity to show that you are familiar with the company, you know what's going on, and you have the skills and knowledge to make you the go-to resource if you are hired. When you are asked if you have any questions, do *not* start asking them about vacation policies and benefits. Ask things like:

- What does it take to be a top performer here?
- What are the company's top priorities in the next year? *Five* years? How could I be a significant contributor to helping you achieve them?
- What would you like to see me accomplish in the first month? First three months?
- I see that [insert name of competing company] is trying [insert what they are doing] to cut into your turf. How are you going to deal with that?

I could give you a hundred of these questions. They are all over the Internet, so search them out. Just for practice.

Don't leave without making it clear that:
1. You WANT the job.
2. You will deliver everything they need you to deliver.
3. You are low maintenance, well liked, and a good team player.
4. You are current, relevant, and always working to learn more.
5. You are endlessly curious, which always puts you at the forefront of change.
6. You adapt well.

Always, always, always say you want the job. Period. It makes the people acquiring talent mad when you don't.

Following Up and Waiting

Following up is not only about being polite and respectful, it's about staying on everyone's radar. There are many templates on what to say, so look them up online or in career guides. Then craft your own version that won't look generic, or like you have copied and pasted it. That first follow-up is to thank them for their time, reiterate your interest, and remind them of something unique that happened during the interview.

Then continue to follow up and touch base. This is always tricky because people are busy and don't want to be hounded or pressured. Say you are still interested and touching base. Ask for an update.

Understand that you might not hear back. There are so many people who have jobs and don't sympathize with those who don't. They don't consider how your life is hanging on what they do or do not do. The more anxious you seem, the less they want you.

I have to do this dance all the time because every speaking engagement is like a potential hire. There are more speakers than there are conferences or corporate meetings. I have to sell the meeting planners on my unique qualities and follow up. These people are bugged constantly by speakers, vendors, conference attendees, committee members, and so on. They want a great speaker. Maybe they haven't made the decision.

I have learned to stay in touch until I get an answer. Even when it is uncomfortable, I stay with it. I might "nudge" a planner by mentioning that I have another inquiry for that date. But until they say "we want you" or "we decided to go with someone else" (the fools!), I will continue to touch base.

If you are told to expect an answer within a certain time frame, you can bet that it's probably not going to happen on schedule. Every time somebody tells me, "I'm supposed to hear by next Tuesday; they are trying to act quickly," I say to myself, "Well, that ain't happening." It is common for that decision to get delayed, often to the point of ridiculousness. It is excruciating, it is not nice, and it can make you resentful of the company. Keep it in perspective. Rudeness abounds. And decisions are often back-burnered for reasons out of the hiring manager's control. It's not the only thing they are dealing with. Decisions are delayed all the time.

At some point, you will be in the position of having to send a "nudge" note. Try to time it so you don't wait so long the employer thinks you weren't interested. Check in, say you know things probably are piling up there, but you were wondering if they had made a decision. Do not nudge immediately after your interview, when you are expecting to hear something. Give it a little time.

Once you are sure you were not selected for the job, check in and kindly ask for feedback. Sometimes you'll get it; sometimes you won't. Even if it hurts your feelings, it will help you the next time.

Finally, it makes good sense to stay in touch with every single person who passed on you. Stay in touch; build the connection. Maybe they will have something for you later and maybe they won't. But they might know somebody who knows the person you need to know.

Salary

When I was twenty-three, my transmission started dying on my very first car and I had to get rid of it QUICKLY. My mom and dad went with me to car shop.

Mom was an aggressive negotiator. Dear Dad was a push-over. We were about to test-drive a car and the first thing my sweet pop said was, "We are in a desperate situation here."

I groaned out loud. "Dad, the price of the car just went up five thousand dollars."

And it pretty much did, so we had to go to a different Toyota dealership in another county. My dad had explicit instructions to keep his mouth shut.

Again, if you are desperate, don't advertise it.

You can see the obvious point here. When someone knows you are desperate, you have no leverage. And if you desperately need a job, it can be very difficult to have the courage to negotiate a salary because the whole process is so risky. You need *something*.

"So what are your salary requirements?" you'll be asked.

If you come in too low, they'll think you are desperate. If you come in too high, they'll think you are either too expensive or you are delusional. How do you figure out the right number?

The Columbia University Business School did a recent study that found applicants who requested nice, round numbers as first offers weren't getting as much money as those who asked for very specific, higher numbers. The company will think you have done your research and know your worth if you ask for $84,225 instead of $84,000 or $85,000. That won't spare you the back-and-forth of counteroffers, but the researchers concluded that the adjustments were smaller when you come in with a solid number. Be specific; get more money.

Find out the range. Shoot for the top of it if you think you are one of the better candidates. Research what the market typically pays for the position. Then say your number.

Here is the thing: you have to say it with confidence and certainty. I do this all the time. If somebody balks at my speaking fee and says, "That's a lot for an hour's speech!" I say, "I can help you find somebody cheaper," and then the meeting planner usually gets all squirrely because the cheaper option makes them want me even more. They don't want second best.

The challenge for someone initiating a comeback is that you might feel as if you are negotiating from a position of weakness and, in some cases, you are.

If you have spent a long time looking for a job, you may be desperate. You may have needed to seek positions well beneath your qualifications. Doing that means you have to convince the company that you will stay in the position and make it work on the reduced salary—which makes many people doing the hiring quite skeptical.

Your first goal is to get an offer. Even a lowball is a sign that they want *you*. They've already spent a lot of time in the process and don't want to start over. They also don't want to have to settle for second best, and they want to get on with bringing their new hire aboard. Your job is to ask for more money, going back and forth until they finally say, "No. We won't be able to do that." That's great news, because you know when you have reached the limit. The trick is to handle these negotiations without turning them off or away from you. Be upbeat, kind, and accommodating. Tell them you'll consider their offer. Then come back with something else. You know how important these negotiations are because every pay increase is based on a percentage of what you are already making. All of your standard annual raises, cost-of-living increases, or preordained percentages of increase for promotions will be based on what you are earning.

Take some time searching online for the average salaries for people in your position. Say you are after a job as director of risk management. Just search for "annual salary for risk management director" in your area. If I were looking for that position here in Tampa Bay, the median salary would be $131,333, and the top 90 percent are being paid $169,994. Many employees have reported their salaries online, so always search for pay information based on the company as well. Do your research and then figure out the right salary to request.

What can they afford? What are they likely to pay? It would be great if you had all of that information available to you, but you don't. The one thing I always, always, always do when negotiating fees is ask for something extra. They give me the number and I say, "Could you get them to go to . . ." or "Will you be able to buy books for all the participants?" Why do I do that? Because a senior executive on a panel I moderated said, "Women will always take the first offer. A man will always ask for more."

That is borne out statistically. A 2018 study by global staffing agency Robert Half reported that nearly 70 percent of men and only 45 percent of women negotiated their salaries. The older they are, whether male or female, the less likely they were to negotiate. Always negotiate! That study reported that, for the 2,800 managers surveyed, 70 percent expected candidates to negotiate. So when you don't, you are probably cheating yourself. You also risk looking like a pushover. Companies want good candidates, not cheap candidates—unless the good candidate comes cheap.

As you negotiate, restate your value. Repeat how much money you saved your previous company or how much you exceeded your goal. Show them that your salary just means more money, productivity, or success for them.

Remember that you can also negotiate time off, bonuses, signing bonus, moving expenses, tuition reimbursement, stock options, work days at home, company car, special training, company phone—whatever. Be creative.

That way, if they say, "We can't pay you what you are currently getting," you have ways to get other things of value.

If you feel you are getting shorted, ask that they give you a review at three or six months where your salary will be reconsidered.

Also, remember: don't ask, don't get. I remember telling one employer, "I currently get four weeks of vacation a year. I'm really attached to them." That was all it took.

Keep turning on the charm during this process. Make sure you repeat how interested you are in the position.

And if the offer is less than what you want but you like the people and the job, figure out if you can make it work with your lifestyle. I've known many people who took significant pay cuts to do something they love.

But there is a number that will be too low for you. That is your "walkaway" number. It is very, very hard to walk away from a sure bet when you don't know when the next opportunity will arise. But sometimes you just can't make their offer work.

When you have bills to pay and you are uncertain about the future, the big questions when choosing a job that isn't exactly what you are looking for are:

1. Do you really want the job?
2. Will this job lead to other opportunities?
3. If it is not the perfect opportunity, is it enough to keep you in the game and serve as a stepping-stone into something better?
4. Will taking the opportunity prevent you from having the time to keep searching for something that will pay you more?
5. How will passing on this opportunity impact your lifestyle, savings, and retirement plans?
6. Is it realistic to expect another offer fast enough to protect your future plans?
7. Will you be better or worse off in a year for having taken the opportunity?

There are many talented people who have had no choice but to take a job beneath their abilities and salary expectations. I can't tell you what to do because every circumstance and offer is different. Listen to your gut. As you go through tough times, be your most confident self. But when you are deciding about an offer that isn't exactly right, opt for being "realistically confident." How realistic is it to expect a better offer in time to save your savings?

I know. Very, very tough stuff.

But at least you are in the game.

18

Get Yourself Hired, Part II

Janice had led a $2 billion sales team and exceeded sales goals by $187 million during the two-year period before her company was acquired and all of its senior leadership let go.

Get this: she couldn't get a job.

Her achievements were extraordinary, and you would think that, once it became known she was available, company leaders would have been racing to hire her first. That didn't happen.

Janice, who did not wish to use her real name, was sixty years old.

It was hard processing the experience of being rejected over and over again.

She corresponded with a popular career coach, who responded with this email:

I'm pretty sure you are not going to like this response, but you asked for my honest feedback. I want you to try to put yourself in the mindset/shoes of the younger people you are talking to. All they hear is you talking about your 30+ years of experience. It's clear you've been stressing that repeatedly in interviews. How would you feel? You might think people would WELCOME that, but for most it just screams, "she thinks she's better than us." For example: You made $400K. They would love to make that much. In their minds, they think "She had her success, now it's our turn." Thus, you have to change your entire approach to how you network and interview. You have to remove their bias by telling them you miss working and just want to contribute. Humility will go a long way. You also need to show them you sincerely feel you'd have a lot to learn from them as well. If you don't, then they will sense it and won't bother to bring you on because in their minds they don't need your attitude. I've worked with a lot of highly successful people like yourself who are unable to put their pride aside. They feel their track records should be worth respect and consideration. However, this is an unfeeling, supply and demand workplace. There are plenty of younger, less experienced, less expensive candidates. And, they don't have the assumption they deserve the job. A harsh reality for sure, but it is reality.

Ouch.

When I read it, I felt the pain my friend must have felt reading those harsh words. But those words were true—and she knew it.

I contacted the blunt person who had written that private email to ask permission to quote it. It turned out to be J. T. O'Donnell, who currently has nearly 2.8 million followers on LinkedIn and, as you can already see, tells it like it is.

O'Donnell is the tough-talking CEO of Work It Daily, an online coaching site that has more than three thousand clients who pay monthly fees for an online career-growth program and e-contact with coaches. I wholeheartedly recommend that site because it gives you powerful, affordable coaching and a clear path to propel you forward quickly without stringing you along so you keep giving them money.

So here is our interview. Enjoy a coaching moment with O'Donnell.

I hear from so many professionals who are struggling in the job-hunting process. What are we getting wrong? All the people who were entry-level workers behind you are now starting to come into the sweet spot of their careers. They have experience, they are taking management positions, and there is still room for them to learn and grow. As a seasoned professional, you can't present yourself as, "I have all this knowledge, all this experience, I am a Jack or Jill of all trades, and I can do anything." You think that says you are going to bring all this value. The problem is, younger professionals see you as somebody who is very set in their ways, has a lot of opinions, and wants to come in and push their knowledge around and dominate the conversation— especially if your colleagues are not as accomplished or seasoned as you. So this is where that perception of age discrimination starts to come into play. Younger workers see you as they see their parents; they see you as somebody who is going to dominate. Millennials were raised in very collaborative environments, where colleagues are teammates and they like to work together. But when you do the "Me, Me, Me Show," it goes against the way that they have been raised to work together. It's a turnoff.

So I take it that backfires in the job-hunting process? You leave thinking, "I crushed the interview; I showed them what I have to offer." You don't get chosen and you wonder why. You get angry and blame age discrimination, but it has more to do with the way you presented yourself and your experience.

What should we do instead?

Listen. Ask questions and help them understand that you are not going to dominate or act like a parent, and you're not going to tell them everything they need to do. Say that you realize their workplace is a collaborative environment and you want to use all your skills and abilities, but say you realize you do not have all the answers. That is what they are looking for. Also, don't be defensive when you walk into a room filled with young people. It's not "us versus them." They will sense that. Go in curious and inquisitive. They are human beings, and this is an opportunity to make friends. They are trying to understand your personality and whether you can be a good teammate.

You are famous for telling people to create an interview bucket list. What is that?

Come up with ten to twenty companies you want to work at, then target your networking on LinkedIn. If I am a recruiter and I am paying for the recruiter fee on LinkedIn, I put in my key words that I am looking for, location, skill sets, and the like. It immediately brings up the most relevant people. You have to optimize your LinkedIn profile as if it were trying to meet the Google algorithm. If you are connected to people at the company—even if you don't know them—it will notify the recruiter. So we teach people to find companies they want to work for and reach out, customizing the connection to say, "Your profile came up when I was researching your company, here is why they are on my bucket list, can we connect?" The person says yes. The minute they say yes, you now have moved up in the world of the recruiter because they will get notified about you when they search. If the recruiter sees that you are connected to five people within the company, do you think they are going to open up your profile and take a look? You betcha. So you should get at least five people from the bucket-list company in your connections.

How do you best convey that you would be a great hire?
I see a lot of seasoned pros go in and they are asked to tell the interviewer about a time when they dealt with a difficult situation. And the seasoned professional goes, "Well I did this and I figured out that and I, I, I, I, I'm amazing." Instead, say, "Here it is what my team and I did. Here's how we came up with a solution." At certain points, you can say you did this or that, but nobody thinks that you did it all yourself. You should talk about your teammates and how they contributed to your success and how you were able to work with them to get the results because that is the truth. That's the intellectual humility and emotional intelligence they want to see. I've heard people say the interviewer was intimidated by them. They'd say, "She's thirty years old and I'm fifty years old and obviously she was concerned I would outperform her and take her job." I ask if they asked the other person about herself or himself. But they didn't, so they didn't bond.

Some people have trouble being interviewed by or having to report to people who are the same age as their kids.
I hear that all the time. But the younger generation makes up half the workforce right now and they're the managers. If you want to stay in the workforce, there's a huge chance that you're going to have to work for someone younger than you.

How should we dress when going to companies that have more relaxed dress codes than we are used to?

The old adage "dress one level higher" still applies. So if you know people will be dressed in flip-flops and shorts, then wear dress pants and an open-collared shirt. If you know it's business casual and they're not wearing ties, then wear a tie. The problem most people over forty have is that casual or business casual feels uncomfortable to them. They say, "I'm just going to dress up anyway." Then they are dressed three levels higher than they should be. You have to show up in khakis if that's what's called for. If you don't know what they are wearing, you can say, "I'm looking forward to the interview. Can you tell me the dress code?" Then go one step up.

What should someone do to explain long-term unemployment gaps or a firing?

Accept some form of responsibility and accountability for whatever happened. HR is taught there are three sides to every story: yours, theirs, and the truth. I've seen a lot of older, seasoned workers go in defensive, saying, "In my defense, they had this going on, this going on, this going on," and that tells the other person, "I don't know how to take accountability and ownership or learn and grow from some of the more powerful things that have happened to me." My advice is to always say, "That's a really good question. I'm glad you asked it. This is one of the most powerful experiences of my life. Not a good experience, but a powerful one. Playing armchair quarterback, looking back, here is what I would have done differently . . ." That's all they want to hear. They want to know you have learned from the experience. They know you couldn't control everything. They know a bunch of it wasn't your fault—it was circumstances. But do you have the emotional intelligence and intellectual humility to be able to sit up and look down from thirty thousand feet and say, "This is what I would have done differently"? Or, "When I saw things going south, I should have looked for a new job instead of trying to grind it out." Whatever it is, show what you learned so it never happens again. That's what they want.

There are people who are fired only because of age bias. What ownership do they have in that?

What they should say is, "I'm glad you asked that, it's a great question, it was an amazing set of circumstances. They let go of fifty people and all were over the age of fifty. So I don't know what the criteria was for the company. Looking back, maybe I could have seen they were restructuring sooner and got my résumé together. I know every job is temporary now and I should always have a résumé together and ready to go. I should have been working on that. And I wasn't networking; I was too busy doing my job. I got blindsided—I own it. It certainly looks like age discrimination, I don't know, but the truth is that I got let go and I got blindsided and I'm going to own that and make sure that never happens again." So, again, take ownership for something. The minute you do, everything else you say becomes more credible.

What if someone with a long gap for parenting or travel or something else needs immediate employment?

Staffing agencies. I would definitely go to a temp staffing agency first because just having one or two gigs under your belt is going to give you an opportunity to put something on your résumé. The agency will assess your skills, and then they are going to do the selling because you are available to work. Nobody is going to care about your backstory. You've got the skills, but the hiring company just says, "Send me someone." The beautiful part about that is stay-at-home moms get in there, do a great job, and then the manager wonders, "How are you even available?" Then they get hired.

How do you coach people to deal with the applicant software that seems to be merciless in screening them out when they apply for jobs online?

Job postings are getting hundreds, and often thousands, of applicants, most of whom are not a fit. There is more competition than ever. And here's the worst part: people who are employed always get picked before people who are not. Those systems are screening you out. My advice is to go around it. You have to. If you see an incredible opportunity and you are an 80 to 100 percent match, you need to mobilize your network and find somebody who knows somebody who works there. They don't have to be your best friend. Weak ties are the number-one way people are getting referrals. Then what you need to do as a seasoned professional is write what we call a *disruptive cover letter*.

What is a disruptive cover letter?

The disruptive cover letter does not regurgitate your résumé. It is you telling the story of how you came to learn about what they do or why the job is important and special to you. Companies need to know that you understand them and want to know you have intrinsic motivation to do the work so that, on tough days, you're still going to get up and come in because you identify with what they do. You identify with their customer base, their services, so you've got to tell the story, and this is where the more seasoned worker can totally stand out. As seasoned professionals, we have more life experiences. So we can tell a great story. We have one client, for example, whose mom was in the hospital dying and when he was there, he noticed a lot of equipment that was there was made by a certain company. The equipment really improved his mom's quality of life in the end. He saw they had a job and wrote a disruptive cover letter. The opening line was, "In the darkest times of my life, as my mom was passing away, your company made the difference . . ." He told the story and said, "That's why I know working with you would be making a difference in other people's lives. My résumé is attached." They see this passionate story about why you feel connected to them, and it is a useful and energetic way of presenting yourself.

How about some résumé tips?

The trend is lots of white space, very fact-based, with no subjectivity. Most seasoned professionals have outdated résumés formats that are in tiny fonts, five pages long, talking about how amazing they are. Résumés are very simple today. You know it's right if they call you and say there's not enough information, so I had to speak to you. Ding, ding, ding! That's the whole point. Your résumé should be white space, white space, simple, simple, simple. No objective statement. No long, wordy paragraphs. It's all about the facts. They just need to know the basics.

Top of the page is your specialty, your top ten skill sets, degrees, certifications, industries, and technologies. Recruiters are given a list of requirements and you have to pass the first cut. All that information needs to be on the top of your résumé. The first six seconds they need to be able to go *check, check, check, check*. When you list your work experience: put your job title first—and bolded. Then the company name, not bolded. They are skimming to look at job title progression. Especially if you are an over-forty worker, your bullet points are fact-based and simplified. No epic novels. One or two lines, top. Quantify everything. How many people worked for you? How many accounts did you have? Numbers are easier to absorb.

What do you think of the online services that score résumés to beat the algorithms so you can make the cut? Not much. So it helps you make it past the applicant tracking system, and eventually your résumé gets to a human being. They look at that formatted résumé and think, "What the heck is this? This isn't a résumé." You still get tossed. If you really want the job, you are so much better off writing the story about your emotional connection to the company or the job, then getting that into someone's hands along with your résumé.

You really love using LinkedIn to advertise your brand. Find articles and videos that you react to and share them, along with your thoughts. Get others to react. That's how you earn your credibility these days. If you spend an hour a day liking and looking at Facebook, peel ten minutes off a day, go over to LinkedIn, find an article, post it, and add one hundred to three hundred words about it, and tag three friends and say, "What do you think about this?" It is the equivalent of going to a cocktail party or a business event and having a conversation on the topic. It's genius. When you do that once a day, Monday through Friday, the repetitiveness creates your brand. Somebody isn't going to see it every day, but if you are following each other and they see you posting on it once a week, six months later when they need to find somebody who knows their stuff about that topic that is showing up on their feed, who are they going to think of? The person who's showing up on their feed. It's like having your own newspaper column or TV show. You're just doing it in small sound bites on your feed.

Valuable advice that you should adapt to present your unique qualifications in the right way for today's job market.

19

Legal Matters

Something's changed at work. The raises stop. Your once-stellar performance reviews are terrible. Your bosses and coworkers treat you like you are suddenly stupid. You get assigned the work nobody wants. You are asked, "When are you going to retire?" You are offered a buyout or laid off.

Is this just a typical rotten time in your corner of corporate America, or is there something more nefarious going on? And what can you do if you are being discriminated against because of your age? What if they are nailing you because you took a leave?

If you are forty or older and you are pretty sure you are a victim of age discrimination . . .

Well . . .

Good luck finding justice.

Wait. Isn't it illegal to discriminate based on age?

Yes.

But age discrimination occurs all day, every day, and it's rare that justice holds the perpetrators accountable. Your first inclination may be, "I'm going to sue!" But successful high-dollar resolutions are uncommon. In fact, low-dollar resolutions are uncommon, too.

It's easier to sue for gender or race discrimination.

One thing I have stressed repeatedly in this book is that there are many times when we could have done a better job insulating ourselves at work by demonstrating our unquenchable thirst for learning and constantly upskilling. If you haven't done that, your employer can blame you for not keeping up with the demands of your job. How do you know whether you are hitting the wall because you haven't kept up or whether you are actually being discriminated against? And what are your options if it really *is* age discrimination?

I interviewed two of the nation's best employment lawyers on the subject.

Suddenly Stupid and Other Discriminatory Tactics

Sometimes discriminatory tactics are quite sneaky, said Donna Ballman, a Florida employment lawyer and author of the book *Stand Up for Yourself Without Getting Fired: Resolve Workplace Crises Before You Quit, Get Axed or Sue the Bastards.*

Older employees are the frequent targets of layoffs. Large employers are usually careful to select people from different age groups so it isn't so obvious, but many times you see far more older ones being pushed out.

"They start asking older employees, 'When are you going to retire?' If you say five years, they want to get rid of you now. They say, 'We are reorganizing.' If the only ones eliminated are older, and the replacements are young, then you have a good case for age discrimination," Ballman said.

Then comes the "suddenly stupid" situation. You've been getting great evaluations for years, but suddenly they are nitpicking and criticizing you, trying to get rid of you for poor performance when you have received great reviews all along.

"That's certainly an indication of age discrimination," Ballman said.

She's seen blatant threats against pensions, with supervisors saying, "If you don't retire, we're going to go after your pension." The threat can make somebody consider retiring immediately because they don't want to lose a vested pension. Most people now don't have that kind of pension—just 401(k)s—so the only thing they can take from them is what is not vested.

Often, before a layoff, employers will approach older employees with an early retirement package.

They'll say, "We're getting ready to do a layoff, but we want to avoid it," Ballman said. Then they make a very attractive offer: "If you turn it down, you can be fired at will."

Other employers might restructure jobs, cut job responsibilities, and isolate you. No more invites to meetings and you are suddenly insignificant.

"I had one where they specifically said, 'Don't go to these networking events because millennials don't want to hear from you.' Usually, it is not that blatant. They just increase the humiliation factor by excluding you, trying to get you to quit."

FYI, it is illegal to deny a promotion just because the company thinks you might retire soon. It is not illegal to ask when you are going to retire, but if it is accompanied by discriminatory action, then there is more to consider.

There are many situations where older workers are denied training under the assumption that they will be leaving soon.

"They'll cut hours and basically force you to quit because you aren't getting paid anymore," she said. "They'll call you 'Old man,' indicating they think you are senile, and just harass you."

There is a perception that older people are slower, less willing to change, and less open to new technology, Ballman said. "I don't think that is necessarily accurate. I think older people are more reliable, are more likely to show up on time, work longer, work harder, learn new things. Yes, I think there is a misperception of age. And then there are people who are truly losing it as they get older. That's not age discrimination. That's an inability to perform their job."

You're Too Expensive or You're Behind on Technology

Can you be fired because your salary is too high? Yes.

"If the employer decides the job description doesn't warrant a particular pay scale, they should explain that to the employee and give them an opportunity to take that lower pay," she said. "Instead, they say, 'You're too expensive.' If they don't give an opportunity to take that lower pay, that would still be age discrimination. If they just say they are cutting pay but not really doing it, that would also be age discrimination."

One way to change perceptions is to accept and seek any and all trainings, especially in technology.

"Be on the cutting edge and you can prove those stereotypes wrong," Ballman said. "Don't sit on your laurels and assume people know what you've done. If you have a younger boss, they have no idea what you did twenty years ago for your company. Don't assume people will respect you just because you have been there twenty years. Make sure people know your accomplishments, and don't expect people to respect you because of the past. You have to continue to be the great employee you always were."

She's had people come to her and, when the subject of trainings comes up, say, "I didn't want to go to that training. I know how to do my job."

If bosses see you resisting training and complaining that the new way is worse than the old way, you are branding yourself irrelevant, not old.

Another thing: if you have a younger boss, you're going to have to deal with it, she said. Buck up. Be good to young people!

It's always a mistake to treat anyone on a lower rung than you with disrespect because that person can rise quickly and easily become your boss, she said.

Avoid advertising your age. There are endless stories of people looking young, and then the boss finds out their age and suddenly they are treated completely differently. Don't talk about age and big birthdays, and don't list your birth year on Facebook.

Women suffer from age discrimination more frequently than men, said Diane King, a Denver lawyer who has successfully tried, arbitrated, and mediated hundreds of employment cases.

"I have long said that older women are the most discriminated-against group," she said. "Especially assertive older women. Companies hire them for their contacts, knowledge, and wisdom, and then chew them up and spit them out."

King said, "The thing that is so bad about federal law is that, under age discrimination, you don't get emotional distress damages if you win." She added, "You can't sue because somebody calls you a dinosaur and says terrible things every day. You can only sue for things that affect your pocketbook. So you have a fabulous career and get terminated right at the end, and you are devastated. You have no emotional distress compensation and you don't get punitive damages. The only remedy besides lost wages you get is back pay doubled. And that back pay is from the time of termination to trial. You just get that doubled, no matter how outrageous your situation was."

King lays out the way to document a case:

- Document if someone makes comments about your age, asks when you are going to retire, gives you a birthday card with a dinosaur on it, etc. Include dates, details, witnesses.

- Save emails.
- Many people tape-record conversations if it is legal in their state. All but twelve states allow "one party consent" for recordings, meaning both people don't have to know a recording is being made. You can search online to see whether your state allows it. In some states, tape-recording without permission is a crime, so be careful.
- Keep copies of all of your evaluations.
- Keep the employee handbook—a gold mine of rules that must be followed.
- Hang on to any physical evidence, which could be anything from a photo left on your desk, inappropriate signs or calendars hanging on the wall, written documents, etc.

King notes that men don't always recognize their firing as age discrimination and often think what happened to them was just unfair or highly political. "They say, 'I was just getting ready to retire and they could replace me with two younger guys, so they fired me.' They don't have the experience with discrimination that women or minorities have. So they don't make the leap in their minds to say, 'Oh. That was discrimination.'"

King says to educate yourself on the warning signs of age discrimination. There is a code for it. People say things like, "We need young blood, fresh out of college, who have the latest skills and know the latest technology," or "We need people who cost less," or even "We need people with energy."

"It all depends on how you say it," she said. "An employer can say, 'I want people who cost less' as long as it is not a proxy for age discrimination. If you are being replaced with a young MBA graduate, well, they don't come cheap. In sales, they have annual meetings and try to hype everybody up. They say they want young, motivated people who want to work 24/7. Sometimes, you look at how companies advertise for employees and all the people in the pictures are young."

When Did You Graduate High School?

For the record, it is illegal to fire someone because of age and it is illegal not to hire someone because of age. Companies are starting to ask secondary questions to figure out age, such as, "When did you graduate high school?"

"Those questions allow them to do the calculations," King said. "We would still have to prove it was being asked for the purpose of discriminating because of age, but why would you ask that question if you didn't want to know how old someone was? If they ask when you graduated college, people can graduate late. So, they ask high school. Who cares about that, unless they are trying to discriminate on the basis of age?"

I've interviewed many older job hunters who are convinced that an algorithm looks at questions like the high school graduation date and immediately rejects their application.

"If that age question is built into the algorithm and they do that, that is clearly illegal," King said. "I would love to have that case. Hiring is a harder area to prove discrimination because people never really know why they didn't get hired. It's either, 'You didn't have this,' or 'You have too much of that,' or 'We hired an internal candidate.' They won't really tell you."

Instead of counting on the law, count on yourself, first.

"It's important not to look old-school," King said. "You have to do things that are innovative and cutting edge and show you are still thinking of new things. If you are going to be discriminated against, you are going to be discriminated against. It doesn't matter how good you are or how much of a rock star.

For years, you are doing well and then you get a new boss and suddenly you are getting dinged in your reviews and getting warnings and then laid off. There is nothing to protect you from that."

Companies also find outrageous ways to get rid of older people.

King filed a federal class-action lawsuit against a company that became upset with health-care costs after the Affordable Care Act passed.

"They decided that, if they became self-insured, they'd save a tremendous amount of money if they didn't have sick employees. It wasn't just the employee being sick, it was the employee's spouse and children. So the first thing they did was encourage employees to test their blood pressure, cholesterol, blood sugar.

"They decided, 'Wouldn't we be clever if we found a way to fire the people with the health problems and say they have performance problems?'" Over a year's time, the company fired hundreds of people. King filed a federal class action against the company, which is still pending.

The problem in all age discrimination cases is that the courts have made it harder to win. You have to prove that the company was absolutely discriminating against you *because* of your age. You have to file a complaint with the EEOC within a certain time frame (which varies by state) and then file suit. State laws may be more favorable to you than federal statutes.

What's especially tough about these cases is that you must prove that your age was what motivated your employer to fire or hinder you. If you were suing for race or gender discrimination, you'd only have to prove it was a contributing factor.

Are they firing you because you are old? Or are they doing it because you are too expensive? There is a difference. They don't have to keep expensive employees.

I know how infuriating all of this is. I know how much you want to fight back.

Years ago, I could have sued my employer for sex discrimination. I had a miserable experience with the terrible boss I described earlier and I wanted to fight back. King, who is one of my heroes, told me that it wouldn't be worth it. First, it wasn't a slam dunk. It didn't matter whether I was right or wrong, or whether I won or lost. That lawsuit would have continued to impact my career. Her advice was to move on.

She said words I never forgot: "Success is the best revenge."

That is so true.

In a perfect world, every wrong would be righted. But it is an imperfect world and the courts aren't doing much to help you if you are the victim of age discrimination. It's not always a dead end, and if you pursue a case, I wish you all the luck in the world.

The Age Discrimination in Employment Act of 1967 (ADEA)

The Age Discrimination in Employment Act of 1967 (ADEA) protects applicants and employees who are forty years of age or older from employment discrimination based on age. It applies to private employers with twenty or more employees, state and local governments, employment agencies, labor organizations, and the federal government. Under the ADEA, it is unlawful to discriminate against a person because of his or her age with respect to any term, condition, or privilege of employment, including hiring, firing, promotion, layoff, compensation, benefits, job assignments, and training. Harassing an older worker because of age is also prohibited. It is also unlawful to retaliate against an individual for opposing employment practices that discriminate based on age or for filing an age discrimination charge, testifying, or participating in any way in an investigation, proceeding, or litigation under the ADEA. The ADEA permits employers to favor older workers based on age even when doing so adversely affects a younger worker who is forty or older.

ADEA protections also include:

- **Advertisements and Job Notices**
  The ADEA generally makes it unlawful to include age preferences, limitations, or specifications in job notices or advertisements. A job notice or advertisement may specify an age limit only in the rare circumstances when age is shown to be a "bona fide occupational qualification" (BFOQ) reasonably necessary to the normal operation of the business.
- **Apprenticeship Programs**
  It is generally unlawful for apprenticeship programs, including joint labor-management apprenticeship programs, to discriminate on the basis of an individual's age. Age limitations in apprenticeship programs are valid only if they fall within certain specific exceptions under the ADEA or if the EEOC grants a specific exemption.
- **Pre-Employment Inquiries**
  The ADEA does not explicitly prohibit an employer from asking an applicant's age or date of birth. However, such inquiries may deter older workers from applying for employment or may otherwise indicate possible intent to discriminate based on age, contrary to the purposes of the ADEA. If the information is needed for a lawful purpose, it can be obtained after the employee is hired.

- **Benefits**

  The Older Workers Benefit Protection Act of 1990
  (OWBPA) amended the ADEA to specifically prohibit employers from denying benefits to older
  employees. Congress recognized that the cost of
  providing certain benefits to older workers is greater
  than the cost of providing those same benefits to
  younger workers and that those greater costs might
  create a disincentive to hire older workers. In limited circumstances, an employer may be permitted
  to reduce certain benefits based on age, as long as the
  cost the employer incurs to provide those benefits
  to older workers is no less than the cost of providing the benefits to younger workers. Employers are
  permitted to coordinate retiree health benefit plans
  with eligibility for Medicare or a comparable state-
  sponsored health benefit.

Family and Medical Leave Act Violations

There are legal matters for those of you who are coming back to
work after taking a leave under the Family and Medical Leave
Act, so I asked King to give us a summary.

First, FMLA applies to companies that have fifty or more
employees within a seventy-five-mile radius. If you qualify for a
leave, you can take up to twelve weeks off every year. They don't
have to pay you, but if it is certified by a doctor, they have to hold
your job for you—unless they were already planning to eliminate
the position.

The law allows you to take twelve weeks of time, but it doesn't
have to be all in one chunk. So if you need to take chemother-
apy on Fridays, you could take every Friday. Or if you have
migraines, you could spread it out for the days when you are

suffering. Perhaps your child has epilepsy and you need to take leave whenever there is a seizure.

Employers don't like those intermittent breaks.

"It can make you unpredictable, and they can try to find other reasons to get rid of you," King said.

But if they come out and say they have to terminate you because you are unreliable because you are taking time at random under the FMLA, you can take them to court.

When you fight back for an FMLA violation, you don't have to show they were trying to discriminate against you. You just have to show you were entitled to FMLA and it was either denied or administered improperly.

The Family and Medical Leave Act

The FMLA entitles eligible employees of covered employers to take unpaid, job-protected leave for specified family and medical reasons with continuation of group health insurance coverage under the same terms and conditions as if the employee had not taken leave. Eligible employees are entitled to:

- Twelve workweeks of leave in a twelve-month period for:
  * the birth of a child and to care for the newborn child within one year of birth;
  * the placement with the employee of a child for adoption or foster care and to care for the newly placed child within one year of placement;
  * the care of the employee's spouse, child, or parent who has a serious health condition;
  * a serious health condition that makes the employee unable to perform the essential functions of his or her job;

* any qualifying exigency arising out of the fact that the employee's spouse, son, daughter, or parent is a covered military member on "covered active duty."

- Twenty-six workweeks of leave during a single twelve-month period to care for a covered service member with a serious injury or illness if the eligible employee is the service member's spouse, son, daughter, parent, or next of kin (military caregiver leave).

If You Think You Are About to Get Fired

If you sense a firing is coming and believe it is the result of discrimination, file a written complaint of discrimination or unfair treatment with HR and your boss before anything happens, King said.

If there are things you need on your computer, print them out and take them to your home. Do not forward them to your home email address, because that transmission may be a privacy violation. But if you are allowed to have it, print it out, she said. You may not be allowed to return to your desk or your computer access might be immediately cut.

Then, if you do get fired, ready yourself to walk out with dignity.

"When you get fired, don't say, 'The hell with you, I'm going to get a lawyer.' Be reasonable. Ask questions. Sometimes they are horrible and get police to escort you out. Don't act badly on the way out. It always works against you. Don't throw a fit or call people names. Just leave."

Then, King laughed, call her.

20

Defrump

Several well-known corporate leaders went off the record during our interviews and said, flat-out, that frumpy-looking men and women are turning people off and need to get serious about their image if they expect others to be serious about their careers. I looked in the mirror and realized that, except for when I am onstage, I'm looking a little frumpy myself.

We've got to up our games.

"Unless you are a genius, your style really impacts how people perceive you," said HR consultant Maureen McGurl, who has a long history as a leader in the C suites of major corporations. "The older we get, the full package is more important. It's always important, but as we age, it is more important."

During interviews for this book, my subjects bared some uncomfortable truths about discrimination and what it takes to be considered relevant and viable as your career progresses. The one thing several leaders were reluctant to be quoted on by name was how looks and weight affect careers.

"A frumpy guy has as many issues as a frumpy woman," one said. "It's not that weight is the only issue. How are you wearing your hair? How are you wearing your clothing? How professional is your image? I know heavy men and women who present themselves very well, and they look like they care about that presentation. You have to care."

One senior leader said, "I have one man here in his late forties whose belly hangs over his pants, his shirt is always wrinkled, and he looks messy every day," he said. "You can't look like that and expect to be advanced or even respected."

Said another: "Be in shape. Unfortunately, you see somebody overweight and you wonder if they are going to have the discipline for the job," he said. "I don't want to be quoted on this, but that is how it is. I don't think I act on this kind of judgment. I think others do act on it."

Gulp. From the author with a lifelong weight issue.

Amy Shea, a sixtysomething branded communications consultant and strategist, really nailed this topic for us.

"I actually think the biggest contribution to 'frumpy looks' is an overall disposition—it manifests in a kind of 'shrinking,'" she said. "We stop walking briskly and looking straight ahead and around us. We scurry. We seem frumpy because we're not fully in our clothes. I've seen women dressed in very traditional sweaters and pearls one might associate with older women, and yet they own it. As Will Smith says in *Men in Black,* 'I make this look good.' Their shoulders are back and they are looking around—not nervously but with interest.

"Watch a really vibrant young man or woman who is not glued to the phone. They take up space. They feel entitled to be in the world and look at things and people going by and whatever interests them. I feel frumpy people have gotten a memo that they are winding down now, and they believed it!"

Shea said a millennial at her office told her, "I saw you on the trail. You walk with so much power, so strong. You walk like an athlete. I want to be brash in a way. Not inappropriate or invasive, but definitely here, taking up space."

So how does she advise you not to be frumpy?

1. "Watch a strong, independent thirty-year-old. Watch how they move and where their eyes go and how they move their hands and what they touch. Watch them in movies, on the street, in your life. Then practice your version of that and see how you feel AND how people react to you.

2. "Stand up and fill up your clothes with your energetic persona. Loose or tailored, it doesn't matter. Clothes should be worn by you, not the other way around.

3. "Don't let the old-person voice take you over. Record your voice and listen to it. Does it sound old? Why? I've had a deep voice my whole life, which always read older. But I try to keep my sentences short and focused now. That reads younger, and it creates a good discipline for getting to the point and not wandering.

4. "Be honest about your makeup, hair, and style. Are you still running a look that is dated? Stop being stuck in the past!

5. "Don't try to overuse new slang and don't keep telling old stories. STAY PRESENT. Young people are present. Be that."

That's a good description for the big picture. I also wanted input from a professional image and style consultant, which led me to Cyndy Porter.

"I wish we could show up naked, because we just let it all hang out and have people accept us for who we are, without any judgment," she said. "But that is not the world we live in. We are hardwired to judge one another first based on how we look. That's known and it's proven. We don't need to be trendy. In fact, that can backfire if we are a certain age because it looks like we are trying too hard. We definitely need to look current and relevant. Frumpy is when your clothes don't fit and they just hang on you, you look like you're wearing clothes that are several sizes too big."

Many wonder if it is safe yet to let hair go gray. She says no.

"If you want to look current and relevant, then going gray is a risk because it will age you. Few people have beautiful gray hair. Most of us have kind of a mousy gray that is not attractive, it doesn't complement our skin, and it's not a good idea."

Porter works with people to incorporate their personal brand into what they wear.

"How you behave and how you show up in the world is uniquely you," she said. She uses avatars to help categorize people into the clothing that fits their bodies *and* their personalities.

"I'm a big believer in the capsule wardrobe where you have a set number of items in your wardrobe. It's not the same for everybody. You may say you hate dresses and you love pants. Somebody else might say, "I hate pants, I wear dresses every day." Maybe you would have a few skirts in basic colors, a few blouses in basic colors, and a few slacks. I teach people who buy into this how to wear every piece five ways. I did the math and if everything can go five ways, you wind up with a thousand outfits, mixing and matching. The idea is that you mix and match and you get more discretionary income to get a more interesting jacket that you may only wear one or two ways but you love it and it's a statement piece and then maybe you get some accessories and some scarves and shoes."

Men may not debate skirts and dresses verses pants, but the combinations are a great way to give more options.

If money is holding you back, find quality consignment shops that sell office-appropriate clothes. There are good ones online, too.

"If you go to your local consignment shop, it's hit or miss,"

Porter said. "If you are online and you have a gazillion pieces, then there's always something for everyone and they have a designer section where you can get premium clothes.

"Eighty percent of the clothes in our closets are never worn, which means it is clutter we don't need," she said. "If you go through it and get rid of that 80 percent, some of it still has tags on it, or you've worn it once or twice. Send it off to an online consignment shop and there's somebody who that piece is perfect for. You get half of its value and can go there and buy perfect clothes for you at a discount."

Men Often Think They Look Better Than They Do

Men are often clueless that they have fashion challenges, Porter continued.

"Men are hard-wired to overestimate their attractiveness," she said. "They don't have the same issue with confidence, so they might have an issue with relevance. They don't get away with being sloppy, but they get away with it more than women do. Society is kinder to aging men than women. My husband is a very handsome man. He has gray hair and a potbelly, but he is still seen as a very handsome man. He is sixty-seven. I'm ten years younger than he is and, if I were thirty or forty pounds overweight and let my hair grow gray, I wouldn't get the same advantage. It's not an equal playing field."

Besides, it is easier for men because they have a uniform. They need a good haircut. The biggest challenge for them is to get clothes that fit so they don't look sloppy. They need to make sure their pants aren't too short or too long.

"The problem I have with both men and women is they don't know what they don't know, and they can't see how they could look different. They can't see the end picture. Because men have confidence, they are harder to convince that they could look better. They think they look fine."

Some Quick Thoughts . . .

- If you've gained weight, put some effort into a tailored, thoughtful look. You can't go around wearing something that looks like a tent. You may think you are hiding your fat, but it makes you look big, old, and matronly. Or if you are a guy, it just makes you look like a slob.

- Whiten your teeth. It's so easy. After a lifetime of coffee, tea, red wine, dark juices (and maybe Cheetos), the teeth get yellow and yucky. Go get some whitening strips. They WORK.

- Get groovy glasses! What do people usually see first when they look at your face? All you need to do is search the Internet for "What is trending in eyeglasses this year?"

- Shoes and purses that are dated can out you for being in a fashion rut. Watch what younger people are wearing and carrying.

- The trick to jazzing up your game is wearing classic styles with snazzy accessories.

- If you are a woman whose breasts are heading down toward her navel, invest in a bra that puts them back where they are supposed to be. If you are a guy with that issue (and there are a few), I don't know what to tell you.

- Go get a good haircut. Something new and stylish. Stop chintzing out on the color and change your style so you look like you still have it going on.

- Always have a nice-looking go-to outfit ready for when you are going out on errands. Usually, fashion fails are the result of a lack of forethought.

Now, if you are like me and none of this comes naturally to you, relax. Someone taught me long ago that you can always go to the store and buy the exact outfit that looks so good on the mannequin, accessories and all.

And if you really want to make it easy on yourself (and can afford it), try one of the online clothing subscription services that match clothes for your taste and body type. You can usually send back what you don't like. There are a number of these services, and the reason they are doing so well is that they take the stress out of looking good.

Once you have the right outfit, walk with confident posture. It makes a huge difference.

As for weight, well, people discriminate against obese people. Just yesterday, I had to yell at my friend's husband for calling a woman "fat"—especially egregious because *he* is at least seventy or eighty pounds overweight. As someone whose weight is always up and down, this really made me angry. But it does tell you how others judge our weight.

I have made a living as a motivational speaker even when I weighed substantially more than I weigh right now. You have to convey a comfort and confidence with yourself if others are going to feel that way about you. We all have seen overweight people who look terrible, as well as overweight people who look great. Whether you are big or small, find something that makes you look good and feel good about yourself.

So go to the mirror and have a look.

What now?

21

Plan B: Be the Boss of You

Is it time for plan B?

You won't have to get past HR and suffer the indignities of the hiring process.

You'll know your boss.

Your boss is invested in your success, as are you.

Plan B = self-employment.

Self-employment means you jump off a high, treacherous cliff and believe in yourself enough to know you can fly.

It can be the most intimidating, scary, risk-filled experience of your life.

The U.S. Small Business Association reported in 2020 that roughly one-third of all new small businesses fail within two years, and half by five years. Eighty-five percent of the businesses that go down blame cash flow.

Fortunately, things have changed so that you can earn income almost immediately if you dive into the gig economy.

I am a firm believer in the Law of Attraction, which means your thoughts manifest your reality. So before you do anything, read the classic *Think and Grow Rich* by Napoleon Hill, or hit YouTube to watch the video of "The Secret."

The thing about self-employment is that, unless you have a cushy nest egg, the risks are great. But so are the rewards.

Let's take a minute to see how people have created comebacks through self-employment.

If You Need Income FAST

Many jobs may not pay what you need or want, but will pay while you are figuring out what you are really going to do.

First, you don't have to start a business that requires a huge outlay of cash. There are countless options, especially since we are becoming more of a gig economy. Gigs mean we get hired one freelance gig or contract at a time.

The good news is that you can go make some money TODAY. Set up an eBay business. Drive for Lyft or Uber. Deliver for Uber Eats. Rent out a room on Airbnb. Find gig freelance work online.

When Dan Bracewell recently retired from his sales director job, he thought he'd try doing some freelance writing via Upwork.com. It was not long before he was making a thousand dollars a month, and that was part-time while he was trying to keep fees low to build up his feedback rating.

The hard part was getting the first assignment, but then the work flowed in.

"I really wanted to get something going," he said. "I sent five proposals, didn't get anything back. Sent ten proposals and didn't get anything. So, it didn't happen in the first day or the first week. It took a couple of weeks, but then I got two or three right away, then I had a dry spell, then I got some more. It is a process."

More than one in four of us are working gigs. Some do it for extra money; others do it for their entire income. There are programmers, lawyers, writers, graphic designers, Uber drivers, pet sitters, phone repair people, virtual assistants, tourist guides, chefs, and a million other options for gig work.

The good thing is, you can get going immediately. A few years ago, I put a house on Airbnb and it literally took thirty minutes to straighten up, take pictures, and get the whole thing online and in business. During Florida's high season, it was bringing in an unthinkable amount every month. It was easily enough to live on comfortably. And, again, it only took a half hour to get that revenue stream set up. You can quickly start pet sitting or driving for Lyft or Uber Eats.

It is so easy to do something that you have no excuse to sit there doing nothing. Think about what you know that you could do as a freelancer and then search online for a hiring platform. I hire people through Upwork.com and Guru.com. Freelancers have quick and easy access to people who want to hire somebody fast, but they have to compete against people from all over the world. Often, there are freelancers on the other side of the globe who will well undercut standard pricing for services, but you will figure all of that out. Bracewell says that, with writing, he has an advantage because many clients want U.S.-based people who know American English.

Beyond gig work, you can also start a business in multilevel marketing, something I frown upon because I have seen hundreds of people lose time and money for very little return. They placed their faith in selling magnets or chocolate or essential oils or even sex toys. Yes, some people make a living doing it. But you must take responsibility for independently researching the company to make sure it is one that will give you a chance. Many of these outfits are pyramid schemes. The first thing you should do is search online with the name of the company and the word "scam." Then search for the name of the company and the word "scheme." Google will tell you plenty.

Create a Portfolio Career

When you have stepped out of the corporate world, consider what you can do to create a portfolio of work.

"It's like when you are in college and you get three part-time jobs and put them together to create income for yourself," said Maureen McGurl, the HR consultant who was a C-suite leader in major corporations.

McGurl coached someone who was out of work to look at her skills to come up with a portfolio.

"She can't find that 'perfect job,'" McGurl said. "She has a bachelor's degree and speaks four languages. I said, 'You're working at Patagonia now. You need more money *now*, so let's think about the things you do that can get you more money *now*. You live in Brooklyn, you speak Russian. Find yourself a job as a tutor. It pays very good money. You can also do some work as a nanny.' Professional women don't necessarily want to do that, but they can be tutors and coaches and put together a number of things to help generate the income they need. With the gig economy, this idea of the portfolio is really going to take off."

What should you put in your portfolio?

"You have to know yourself," she said. "Look at what your skills and experiences are and look at what is available today against that. It is different from looking for that single job, and I'm not saying you should not do that. But there are other options today that make sense for you and can generate the income you are looking for."

McGurl has done that herself, between her successful HR consulting business and coaching others.

One of the benefits of a portfolio career is that you are free to take on interim assignments for projects people in your network might know about. She said new firms are launching to help connect talent with short-term assignments.

Getting Real

And, as you do, think about the plan B that will really sustain you. What is it that you see yourself doing in the long term?

I want to share the stories of a handful of people who have hit the wall and rebounded by betting on themselves. For them, plan B was to take charge and run their own business.

Lisa Devereaux had a unique entrance into entrepreneurship. She had won $37,000 on Super Password, and that became a nest egg for her to build what she calls her "Pooki-do fortune." Devereaux, who is simply fabulous, explains that a Pooki-do was "hair accessories extraordinaire." They were a piece of fabric with a piece of polyurethane wire inside and could twist hair into several different hairstyles with complete ease and no bobby pin to hold it down.

Oh, look, let's just fast-forward this story because she sold hundreds of thousands of those little hair doodads that cost just $1.90 to produce and sold for ten bucks each. She made a ton of money in it; because the crowds were so big at trade shows, she was discovered by the QVC shopping network.

Then she got married and went into semiretirement. She'd go on QVC every so often, but when the Pooki-do cycled out, she didn't know what to do with herself. Then her husband told her he was having an affair and wanted a divorce.

"I suddenly realized I was on my own again," she said. She fell into a severe depression, which put her into serious debt.

Pooki-do wasn't going to pull her out of it because there were so many knockoffs that there was no money in it any longer.

Then she saw a scarf that had a slit in it that would help the wearer tie it easily. Devereaux looked at it and realized that the design wasn't right. She modified it, sewed elastic into it, and then realized she had something: a snazzy scarf that didn't take a mechanical engineer to tie correctly.

"No one would ever need to know how to tie a scarf again," she said. She found her fabric and manufacturer, then went into production. She took her scarves to her old buyers at QVC, and they loved them. She sold about eighty thousand of them for $29.99 each—the manufacturing cost was $3.

She had been on QVC for years when her rep called her in 2014 and said that her QVC buyer had been fired and the network was not going to reorder the scarves.

"My heart sank," she said. "I knew I still had inventory there and they, at least, let me sell that off."

But she also had an enormous inventory of unsold scarves at home. She would slowly sell them to individual boutiques, but that wasn't paying her bills.

"I was devastated when I was canceled on QVC," she said.

She'd just moved to Florida and was trying to market herself as an interior decorator while selling scarves to Florida boutiques, but she realized, "These scarves are not going to cut it for me."

"In good times, I'd take home over a quarter of a million dollars and, suddenly, I didn't have any money for anything," she said. "I had a boatload of inventory I had to deplete. When I was on QVC, I was selling thousands at a time. But when you make $5 on an order that you fulfill yourself, you have to re-evaluate your life. The debt was overwhelming me. I felt myself spiraling into another depression. It was devastating and humiliating. I felt like a failure. I looked back and thought, 'What have I done?' I saw my friends with great homes taking fabulous trips. And I was looking at $70,000 to $80,000 of debt and wondering what I was going to do. It scares me to think of how much credit card interest I have paid over these years. It would terrify me if I saw it."

Friends urged her to declare bankruptcy, but she wouldn't even consider it.

"It wasn't the right thing to do," she said. "Everyone told me I should, but I thought, 'I got myself into this and, by God, I am going to get myself out of it.' I worked really hard to have a really great FICO score. My massive debt lowered my score, but now my score is back up, I am out of debt, and I bought myself a house."

How'd she orchestrate that comeback?

You can always bet on what you do best, and what Lisa Devereaux does best is sell. She knew she needed an item with a higher price point than scarves, so she did what a lot of people do.

She got her real estate license.

That was terrifying because her instructor told her to anticipate waiting six months for her first closing, and said she should have a six-month nest egg to cover her expenses before doing it. They said that she'd close two houses the first year, five at the most.

Devereaux closed seventeen.

"I know how to sell something I love," she said. "It's easy. I am very empathetic with my clients. I want them to have their perfect home. I know interior decorating, which adds a lot of value for my clients. I can tell if something is going to be a money pit or easily restored. The one-on-one sales from the women's shows absolutely helped.

"Right now, things are going nowhere but up. As low as I've been in the past, I know life is a roller coaster for me. It goes down, but it comes right back up," she said.

Cleaning Out the Closet

Austin Zakari dove into eBay after a divorce. Over the years, it had been a great resource for selling graduate schoolbooks and, with a divorce on the horizon, provided a quick way to open an instant business.

The first things to go? Items left behind by her ex-husband. "I decided to sell them, more in anticipation of moving than of making money," Zakari said. "I thought, 'Well, this is a lot easier than I anticipated. I liked the idea of having my own business, on my own time and my own schedule. I liked not having to report to someone every day. I wanted something flexible that could be done on my time and shaped to my interests."

It was profitable from the start.

"It grew so big, it became my business," she said. "I ramped it up, hired someone to help me take pictures and come up with a system." Facebook and YouTube were great sources of tips and strategies.

In the beginning, grabbing unused items around the house was an easy source of quick revenue. Clothes, pots, pans, shoes— they'd all sell, so she would go out to thrift shops and garage sales looking for similar items.

As an anthropologist, Zakari is attracted to the stories behind items. Estate sales were great resources of the history behind the products, with family members saying where their mom or dad found something.

She met another eBayer who supported herself for a year selling bras to women who'd gotten enormous boob jobs. The bras are hard to find.

"There is a saying that the riches are in the niches," she said. "Where there is a need, there is a niche."

Zakari works thirty to forty hours a week, selling about a

hundred items a week and clearing about six thousand dollars a month on eBay. Two helpers make it happen.

"You literally can do this out of your spare bedroom," Zakari said. "That's what most people do. This gave me a lot of security. Anybody can do this and it's just a matter of spending time before you start. Watch the videos before you pull the trigger and lay out a plan. And if you need cash today, jump in and learn as you go."

Count on Yourself as Your Biggest Asset

Rene Johnson has had a number of careers, ups, downs, a well-timed firing, four marriages, and some unbelievable success.

She has run businesses all over the country and wound up in my town of Dunedin, Florida, over a decade ago when she opened a gift shop in the quaint downtown area. Her husband wished her well and told her all she had to do was break even.

"To this day, I resent people who start a business as a hobby and do it half-assed because it hurts the community," she said. "I proved him wrong. I did just fine, even at the beginning."

One day, her daughter noticed that the new deli that opened on the edge of downtown had already gone out of business.

"Why don't you buy it and I'll manage it for you?" her daughter asked.

A new, crazy challenge that excited Johnson.

Six weeks after signing the lease, they opened the Living Room—and even managed to get a full liquor license.

"It was insane," she said. "If I am interested in something, I don't ever stop."

It was an instant hit. "But, I could tell we weren't going to be super profitable without more parking and walk-in traffic," she said.

One night, the owners of an Italian restaurant in the best location in town packed up and left in the middle of the night. Johnson thought, "Oh my God, I've got to lease that building."

She tracked down the building owner through county records, and by that weekend she had redesigned and was rebuilding the Living Room's new location at night so it would open—get this—twenty-eight days later. "We moved stuff around entirely, painted, got a new liquor license, had to build and equip the whole kitchen, and then we reopened and immediately had a *huge* spike in business."

They then opened *another* restaurant, the Dunedin Smokehouse, in the original location. Soon, she had an opportunity to move that right next to the Living Room. They were the premier restaurants in town.

Two restaurants and a shop, all at once, from someone who a year earlier had only dined in restaurants. She kept her shop until someone wanted to buy it from her.

Two years later, the restaurants were in the black.

Eventually, someone made her an offer to buy the restaurant. She sold in an owner-financed deal, but the buyers defaulted.

"It was crazy, totally crazy, and we had to fight to get it back," she said. "I missed the Living Room so much, I rehired the people he'd fired and realized that, even though I was really good at it, it wasn't what I wanted to do for the rest of my life."

Then a well-financed buyer came along and bought it.

"Suddenly, I had no businesses," she said.

So she opened Our House, a really eclectic and popular gift shop.

I love her fearless agility. She's willing to try things she knows nothing about. She's run weight-loss centers for Nutrisystem and Jenny Craig and a body-toning and tanning salon, done interior design, sold real estate, and more.

"I've never been afraid to fail because I never thought I would," she said. "I always thought that, if I did something, I would make it work. If something doesn't work out, I don't dwell on it. I always look forward. The only thing you can really count on is yourself. Count on yourself as your biggest asset. You'll have more regret not trying, so just do it. Even if you fail, it is still okay. You just do something different."

Winning, Once Again

Speaking of different, meet Jennifer Argie.

"I'm pushing fifty, and redefining myself as an entrepreneur was a big challenge for me," said Argie, founder of Jenny's Baked at Home. "Huge."

She's not selling cupcakes. She's selling CBD. Hemp.

Fifteen years ago, she created a modern children's furniture line that was so successful, it was in big-box stores like Walmart, Bed Bath & Beyond, and Babies"R"Us. With factories in China, Vietnam, and India, she still couldn't keep up with demand.

Then a dramatic, unexpected battle with a factory in China led to her company being dissolved, and Argie's dream was in pieces.

The loss of a business is a loss of identity, she said.

"But what didn't kill me made me stronger," she said. "They gave me the best lesson in my life. I would love to have sold my business, but I am an entrepreneur. If I did it one time, I could do it again."

Then came a divorce.

Then the breast cancer diagnosis.

She was a single mom with three children.

During treatment, she started looking at cannabis as an alternative for pain management. She couldn't find any healthy edibles, so she made them for herself. She decided to do a Kickstarter fundraiser for her baking mix, and it posted the day before a double mastectomy. She thought she'd have at least a week to recover, but the first week in a Kickstarter is the most important because it's when the momentum has to build. "I got out of anesthesia and said, 'Give me my laptop.' I haven't had a reprieve—ever."

The business has soared and expanded from baking mixes to oils and creams. But she's faced one obstacle after another, particularly when seeking financing in the beginning. Since CBD is a cannabinoid, federal rules kept banks from doing business with the cannabis industry. Since there is no THC in what she creates, she rebranded as hemp.

When she started, she used the bottom two floors of her Brooklyn brownstone as an Airbnb to give her money to run her business. Her thirteen-year-old son came in and said, "This is cute, Mom. I think it's time to get a job." She answered, "Honey, give me another year. I will show you I know what I am doing." She knew she had thick skin and serious passion.

Customers started telling her that the products were helping them with everything from skin rashes to arthritis.

"I was hearing stories of gratitude all the time," she said, "And that is what fired up my passion."

She's winning, once again. Actually, she's really winning. During the COVID-19 crisis, business increased 500 percent.

Lessons from a Master

Before you decide what you want to do, listen to David Cummings, a business innovator and startup genius whose story tells you to dive in, expect a few messes, and just go for it.

Cummings says his story is the routine software-entrepreneur story.

"I started a software company in my dorm room. It went pretty well, made a little bit of money, and that led to an idea for another software company to make it easier for businesses to market their companies online. I started that when I was twenty-seven. We grew rapidly, signed a thousand customers, and, when I was thirty-two, we sold it for $100 million to what became Salesforce.com."

That's a winning-the-Powerball kind of story. And he was just getting started. He bought a one-hundred-thousand-square-foot building in the financial district in Atlanta and turned it into the fourth-largest tech hub in the company, housing three hundred startups with a thousand people. He invested in twenty-seven different software companies, including SalesLoft, Terminus, and others, and those companies have gone on to raise hundreds of millions of dollars in venture capital. Some are doing very, very well.

When we talked, he was thirty-eight years old.

"My mistakes are too many to list," he said. "There is an old adage that 'Many more entrepreneurs die of indigestion than they do of starvation,' and that is true. Entrepreneurs are known for chasing the shiny object and bouncing from idea to idea. But the importance of figuring out distribution for a product in this day and age is just as important as the idea itself. It's always been competitive out there, but the Internet has made it hypercompetitive, so customer acquisition has become much more difficult. But, at the same time, when you crack that nut, the scale of success can be so much greater."

He breaks down the business world very simply. On the consumer side, a product has to fall into one of the seven deadly sins (pride, envy, gluttony, lust, greed, sloth, or wrath). Otherwise, "it's probably going to fail."

On the business side, it has to do one of two things. It either has to be in the path of revenue, or it has to be mission critical to a company, so the company has to use it in order to run the business.

"Most entrepreneurs fail for a variety of reasons, but many fail because they make a "nice to have" product, not a "must have" product, and it's only 10 percent better than what else is on the market, not ten times better. We refer to this as the difference between painkillers and vitamins. Too many entrepreneurs are making vitamins when the real opportunities for success are the ones making painkillers."

For a product or a company to have staying power, it has to offer long-term value.

For you to have staying power, you have to be a doer, a self-starter who is willing to break down barriers and walk through walls, he said. "Being an entrepreneur is being able to figure things out on the fly. One of the main reasons startups do better than some of the large companies is because of how fast they can operate. They don't have the bureaucracy and approval process, the long delays to get things done. If you are not an action-oriented doer-type who likes to break things along the way, it's not likely that you will be successful. Someone who likes to get things done quickly adapts on the fly. You have to make decisions absent information. There is a lot of analysis paralysis and a desire to make the perfect decision, but you have to make decisions and get things done.

It can also take a lot of patience and rejection. Cummings said most successful entrepreneurs were not successful with their first idea.

"It's tough to be so introspective that you can say, 'My baby is ugly and I need to go a different direction.' By that time, many are so worn out they say entrepreneurship is not right for them."

A lot of entrepreneurs start hitting the wall and have to figure out what the problem is. Is it the idea? The timing? The market? Is it resources?

"Most of the time, people want to give up because the idea they fell in love with wasn't the idea that would be commercially viable and they were going to have to pivot," he said. "Are they going to do that or are they worn out?

"It is never easy," he said. "Sometimes, people catch lightning in a bottle at the right place at the right time and someone says, 'I need this thing and I will pay for it.' The entrepreneur takes them up on it and their timing was impeccable. But that is a one-in-ten thousand situation."

Why I Love My Boss

I love my boss. She lets me come in late. Or if the weather is great and I am not on the road, she might say, "Maybe you should go kayaking today instead of working." But the real reason I love my boss is that she knows when I need to ratchet it up, work late into the night, make calls I don't want to make, or study something new. I love my boss because nobody can manage me better than I can manage myself. I absolutely love being my own boss.

I was quite nervous when I left my career as a newspaper editor and reporter and became a self-employed, starving author. I knew it would be tough because I was easily distracted and a little undisciplined. I made an agreement with myself that I would change those qualities by making lists of tasks and goals to keep me on track. My mantra was (and still is), "Self-employment is a privilege that must be earned." These are my principles:

1. Make up your mind and commit.
2. Have a list of goals for each day and week to keep you on track and more productive.

3. Whenever you hit a wall, look at your business plan to see what is not working. Either you need to tweak the plan or write a new one.

4. Expect obstacles. They are inevitable. Weak people see obstacles and stop. Strong people see obstacles and always find a way.

5. If you don't believe in yourself, no one will believe in you.

6. You never know how close you are to turning the corner until you turn the corner.

7. Don't waste money on *anything* you don't NEED.

8. Always live beneath your means. I never spend this year's earnings until next year.

9. Just enjoy the roller coaster!

I know so many people who have dreamed of seizing their own power and doing what they always wanted to do, but they lacked the guts because their kids were in school or they didn't have the confidence or the timing wasn't perfect or whatever. I tell you, there is never a straight shot up to the top. You will always have good and bad years, and just when you think it is going to get easier, it gets harder.

But what if I hadn't bet on myself? I'd have continued living by the rules and priorities of others. I would have missed out on the joy of succeeding despite so many awful obstacles that seemed to be telling me I was going to fail. I would never have known what I was capable of if I hadn't had the guts to jump off that cliff.

I have honestly never had a single bad day of work since I left my job at *The Tampa Tribune* in 1999. Not one. I have dealt with some really tough challenges, but I have had so much fun and joy doing what I love.

A few years after I'd gone off on my own, I ran into an old colleague who told me, "Everybody thought you were crazy when you did that."

Maybe I was. But what a ride it has been.

For me, plan B was the only way.

22

Plan C: You Can Always Downsize and Pull a Krakel

And now for plan C, the "nuclear option." This is where you can say, "The hell with it," figure out your budget, downsize, and just go live your life without going back to work.

You may wonder how this fits in a book about getting your career back on track. Well, sometimes you realize the best option is to stop trying to force it so hard and go live the life you want. In that way, you are "coming back" to your truth.

The trick is to find your own way of "pulling a Krakel."

Dean Krakel is a close friend of mine. He's become my hero and guru, too. We go waaaaay back to when I was a reporter at the *Rocky Mountain News* and he was a photojournalist who chronicled the wild West.

When the *Rocky* went out of business in 2009, things got rough for Krakel. He'd recently divorced, which devastated his finances and his spirit. The paper went under. Then this nationally acclaimed photojournalist found himself cooking in a Chinese restaurant, cutting timber, and working construction. He wound up in bankruptcy court. He lost his house in a short sale, and his car was repossessed.

His sister told him, "You aren't your car, you aren't your house, you aren't your things. You have to separate yourself from any of that. To find out who you are, you have to get on the edge of things."

He ended up getting hired by the *Rocky*'s competitor, *The Denver Post,* a once-fine newspaper that has suffered greatly as the newspaper industry has collapsed, with endless layoffs and buyouts. In 2015, the *Post* offered employees another buyout.

Krakel shocked everybody when he accepted it. At sixty-two, he was ready to take a hike.

The 550-mile Colorado Trail had been calling to him for years. This was his chance.

"I didn't get much of a buyout," he said at the time. "Just enough to get me through the trail a couple of months. Sometimes you have to jump and build your parachute on the way down."

The way he has built his parachute in the years since has caused many of us who know him to reevaluate much in our lives and careers. Krakel's choice proves there are other rewarding, viable options that don't entail walking the path you always thought you would travel until the end of your career.

It comes down to your things.

It costs a lot of money to maintain your things. You have to store your things, heat and cool your things, and insure your things. When you get rid of your things, you don't need as much money to live. Then you can go do fun stuff with the time you have by not working so hard to maintain your things.

Someone long ago told me, "Less money equals more living."

After finishing the Colorado Trail, Krakel went back to the *Post,* but was laid off as he eyed an even bigger hike—the Continental Divide Trail, from New Mexico to Canada.

He hiked 1,242 miles of the 3,100-mile trail, and plans to head back up to finish. The trail is unthinkably rugged, traversing the highest altitudes and leaving the three hundred people who attempt it each year exposed to the most dangerous elements. Krakel described crouching on his toes on a bare mountaintop as lightning cracked all around him.

He made a decision to further downsize, let his son rent his home, and move to the scenic mountain town of Crested Butte.

"I woke up about 2:30 in the morning, and there were dishes in the sink," he remembered. "I'd already minimalized everything and I was washing dishes and I was wondering, 'Why am I washing these dishes? I don't need them.' I walked outside and threw them all away, except I kept one coffee cup, two tall glasses that I like, two small glasses, one large plate, one small plate, one knife, one fork, one spoon. I had a box of sharp knives. I counted them. I had sixteen. I decided I'd pick my favorites. I had six. Then I started throwing things out. I split the box of what I was keeping and made it smaller. The last morning it was like, 'I don't need any of this shit. Why am I taking it to Crested Butte? I am done packing and carrying all of this stuff with me.'"

The hardest downsizing involved the mementos from his travels: rocks, shells, tree bark, knickknacks that he'd accumulated from his travels. "My whole fireplace mantel was covered in them. There were buddhas, Indian deities, skulls, bones, things from Africa. I went through my closet and found a box of valuable artifacts I'd moved from my last move. Then I found another box of sacred objects. I thought, 'This is crazy.'"

He went through everything. He'd pick up an object, and if he had a memory of or feeling about it, he kept it. Everything else went into the "disregard box." After that, he knew which objects were valuable to him. The next day, he did it again, winnowing down his treasures until they fit in one box.

"At the end of the day, the disregard box went into the garbage with the blender and all the other things that had no meaning," he said. "Now I have a little box of sacred objects that is very valuable to me."

Hardest to toss were his photographic images. Krakel has won many, many awards for photojournalism. He is the author of three books, and his photos have appeared in *National Geographic, Rolling Stone, Outside, Time, Newsweek, Life,* and other magazines. As a photo editor, he was part of three Pulitzer Prize–winning photo teams.

He had tens of thousands of prints, negatives, and slides.

"I went out to my shed and there were four Rubbermaid tubs full of slides and negative sheets, all rubber-banded. They have been in the shed for five years, and they were in a garage two years before that," he said.

His life's work.

"And I thought, 'You know what? I'm done with it. Like somebody is going to come to me and say, "We want to do a photo book on your trip to Yellowstone thirty years ago"? That isn't going to happen.' I had boxes and boxes and boxes of newspaper clips," Krakel said. "Clips from the *Rocky Mountain News* and even the *Pinedale Roundup.* I had clips from everything I'd ever published or written. I was like, 'Why am I hauling all of these things around? Am I going to write a résumé and say, "Here is something I did thirty years ago"? Nobody cares about that stuff.' Are my boys going to go through ten thousand slides after I die and look at all those sheets? No, they aren't. Are they going to look at yellowed newspaper clippings and magazine stories? No, they aren't. When my mom died, her stuff was a burden. It wasn't fun. I'm not going to do that to my boys. I'm going to go out with as little as possible."

He tossed it all.

Then came a freak-out.

"I thought, 'My God. You've totally messed your life up . . .' Then the *Post* called and asked if I wanted to work a few months during the Broncos season."

The job would have given him money that would replenish the savings he'd gone through.

"I was thinking, 'You could have stayed in your house, kept all your friends, had a job throughout the winter, had a place to stay all winter, but instead, you have just cut the plank out from under yourself.'"

He chose Crested Butte.

"All we do is support our stuff," he said. "We have a house, we have a car, but we don't have it. We are renting them from the bank. Our stuff begins to own us. My kids are grown. I want to have experiences, not stuff, not things. There is a lot less time in front of me than behind me. What am I going to do with what I have left? When you give things up, you are able to find out who you are. It is easier to sleepwalk. It is not easy to be awake. I'm not saying I'm awake, but I don't think I am sleepwalking anymore."

Many people fear his kind of risk.

"A lot of people can't quit their jobs and walk away from things," he said. "A lot of people won't."

But those photos he posted of his trips—of what he saw and did—were so humbling. Three months on the Colorado Trail cost him five thousand dollars. How much do you spend in three months? And are you doing anything as cool as that?

Krakel bought a mobile home, and every photo he posted on Facebook during that endlessly long winter was filled with tons and tons and tons and tons of snow.

"One of the best winters of my life," he said. "It took nearly all the savings I had left. I back right up to a national forest, I've got a great canyon to bike ride up right out my door, a river to float and hang out by, a mountain to bike and run and hike up, and I seem to be making new friends and creating community. I'm living a healthier life, more active, and the amazing thing is there's work here for different publications. I am so blessed and grateful."

He then sent me a photo of the mountain river out his back door, followed by a photo of what he left behind a year ago in the *Post* newsroom.

He is currently in training to bike about a thousand miles of the Continental Divide through Colorado and Wyoming.

I want to go with him.

Which Brings Us to the Tourist and the Fisherman

His experience leads me to this very well-known parable written by the late German author Heinrich Böll, who won the Nobel Prize in Literature in 1972. In Böll's story, a tourist sees a fisherman asleep in his boat in a gorgeous European fishing village. When he takes the fisherman's picture, the sound of the shutter wakes the man up.

"Why aren't you out fishing?" the tourist asks.

The fisherman explains that he'd already gone fishing and caught four lobsters and a couple of dozen mackerel. "I have enough for tomorrow and even the day after tomorrow," he says.

The tourist pushes him to imagine what he could catch if he'd go out fishing again, or if he went three or four times. What a haul he'd have! Or imagine what he'd get if he did that every day; why, he'd make so much money he could buy himself a beautiful new boat, and in a few years he could even afford a trawler. He'd catch so much fish, he could have a store, a smokehouse, a marinating factory. Then he could have many restaurants and even ship his fish to restaurants in Paris.

"What then?" the fisherman asks.

"Then you may relax here in the harbor with your mind at ease, doze in the sunshine—and look out at the magnificent sea," the tourist says.

"But that is what I am doing right now," the fisherman says.

Conclusion

I learned plenty back in 2009 when I met a man whose business was about to collapse.

He was the producer of an event, and I was the keynote speaker. Everything was *perfect* that day. His production was flawless: the AV, the graphics, the event timing—everything. He'd laid out glow-in-the-dark tape to illuminate my path from the green room backstage to the stairs beside the stage.

Afterward, I told him I was impressed. I'd never seen anything like it.

"This is the only event I have booked for this year," he admitted. "I am fighting for the right to do the work that I love."

That was his challenge during the hardships that hit his business and many others during the Great Recession. Many people suffered greatly. Many people saw their businesses go under.

So you've hit a wall and now must decide whether you will fight for the right to do the work that you love.

You can either surrender in frustration or fight until you climb over the wall.

You can't win unless you fight. Be relentless.

Make up your mind.

What do you need to learn? Learn it.

Who do you need to meet? Meet them.

How many times do you need to try? As many as it takes. Even if you get kicked around so many times you want to quit, always, always get back up and try again. My motto is the old Japanese proverb: "Fall down seven times, get up eight."

Life used to be so easy. I'd leave the office for lunch and come back to a little pink slip of paper that said, "While you were out . . ." Either I called the person back, or I didn't. I would go home after work and I didn't have to answer the phone for work calls; I didn't have to check email to see if my boss needed to remind me to do this or ask me about that. Life was so simple.

No home computer, so no after-hour emails. No cell phone, so no text messages.

BAM!

Everything changed for us. Every single thing. The skills we graduated college with are mostly out of date. Younger people are taking charge, and they don't have even a quarter of our experience. This is just not what any of us expected.

A couple of years ago, I spoke to the young lawyers' division of the Florida Bar Association. There I was, over fifty, and when I looked out at these young lawyers—all of whom were thirty-six or younger—I said, "Go ahead and judge me for my age. But I believe in reincarnation, and by the time I am your age, you are going to be pooping in your Depends."

They roared with laughter.

I love that story because, whatever biases we are facing, younger people will likely face them when it is their turn. There is always somebody newer and smarter who will be the next big thing.

No career is a straight shot upward. It's always up, down, hot, cold.

Good years and bad years.

It is always a fight to do the work that you love.

I was just thinking about that show producer I'd met all those years ago and decided I needed to track him down to get the end of the story. I searched through endless emails from 2009 and found him. We just got off the phone.

His name is David King, owner of the Carlin Company.

He remembered that event in Orlando so well because the convention industry completely tanked during the recession. Many, many conferences were canceled. Once-lavish annual events were cut to bare bones. That one show in 2009 was his career lifeline.

"That particular show, it was a comeback," he said. "It saved us from disaster. We needed the money, and we needed it badly. We killed ourselves to do a good job. After that, our business roared back."

The comeback lasted for more than a decade. Then he hit another rough year. But King knew that, again, there was a way to fight back.

"You have to keep a successful thought dominant in the front of your head at all times," he said.

There is a lot of wisdom in that man.

Change is exhausting. The mere science of what is presented to us on a daily basis is overwhelming. But we are either victims or we are warriors.

You will get where you need to go if you keep taking the next step forward. Fear creates more fear. Stress creates more stress. Worry creates more worry. Don't freak yourself out—just keep moving forward.

Don't judge your success by what you accomplished with ease. Judge it by the person you became when things got rough.

You are not your job, and you never were.

You are fighting for the right to do the work you love.

Acknowledgments

To my mom and dad, because I miss them so much.

To Kathy Casey, who kicked me in the ass and made me finish.

To Julie Hipp, Rebecca Whitley, and Geoffrey Roth, the three who have loved me the most and who have always been there.

To Jim Germer, my big brother, who is my friend, and his wife, Jeannine Germer, who is such a great sister-in-law.

Extra thanks to Jayne Bray who helped proof this. I cannot write a book without my sis.

To Pamela Harty, my agent, my fabulous, fabulous agent, who is so good at what she does and is such a great human being.

To George Witte, my editor, who is an uplifting, brilliant man whom I love working with. I am so grateful for your support.

To the rest of our team at St. Martin's Press: Brant Janeway, Erica Martirano, Kevin Reilly, Laura Clark, and Leah Johanson, who I fell in love with on the first minute of the first Zoom call.

To my publisher, Jennifer Enderlin, who actually read my unsolicited email and matched me up with George.

To my posse: Joyce Duarte, Cindy Cole, Tina Proctor, Kathy Bowers, Heather Gracy, Dana Kuehn, Lisa Kruckeberg Alfe, Julia Jenkins, Jason McKeever, Austin Zakari, Lisa Devereaux, Donna and John Larson, Shane and Dan Bracewell, Malea

Guiriba, Teresa Lawrence, Martha and Ed LeMasters, Granny Vicki Smith, Kathy Witt, Doug and Teri Swift, Monica Kok, Jayne Bray, Oma Helga Borsch, Jackie St. Joan, Brian Campbell, and Jeanne Elliott.

To Linda Mary Lindsay, one of my sisters in life, whose death still leaves a big hole in my heart.

Thanks to every news editor I ever had, who made me a better journalist by teaching me to welcome input and criticism. Thanks to my colleague Debbie Frazier, who taught me the truth is one more phone call away, advice that has helped me so many, many times.

To my old team that got this author thing started. My first book editor, Jennifer Repo, and my old agent, Caroline Francis Carney, who both pushed me toward my dream and became lifelong friends. Sad you left publishing, but so happy you are happy.

Finally, to my faithful pets throughout my life, who got and get me through *everything*. They think I am perfect. To my dog, Sonny, and cats Coconut and Teddy, who are right here as I write this, and to the many pets who have passed. Perfect, unconditional love. Well, except that I know Sonny would trade me for a single Cheeto, then wonder where I went. It's all good.

Index

About the Author

FAWN GERMER is the acclaimed bestselling author and keynote speaker who will reach inside of you and pull out your best self. This popular TEDx speaker teaches you to dive into change, relevance, and viability.

Germer once had a bully boss tell her that she'd never be more than she was at the time—a reporter—and she sure showed him. She is a four-time Pulitzer-nominated investigative journalist and the bestselling author of nine books, including the Oprah pick *Hard Won Wisdom*.

Germer has interviewed more than three hundred of the most accomplished leaders of our time, including U.S. presidents, Olympic athletes, CEOs, prime ministers, Academy Award winners, and many other trailblazers who shared with her the secrets of true success.

From them, she learned that success is born out of risk and that power comes from a self-awareness that disables the issues of doubt and self-esteem.

Her first book was rejected by every major publisher in the United States, but Germer persevered until it was a bestseller that Oprah held up and called "very inspiring."

She is one of America's most sought-after leadership and motivational keynote speakers and webinar leaders and ranks thirteenth on the prestigious Global Guru's list of Best Leadership Speakers worldwide. She travels the globe with her message of viability, performance, and power. She has keynoted for Coca-Cola, Kraft, Ford Motor Company, Cisco, Pfizer, Hallmark, Deloitte, Kimberly-Clark, Xerox, Bayer, AIG, Novartis, GlaxoSmithKline, the Network of Executive Women, Harvard, the UCLA Anderson School of Business, the Wharton School of Business, and many others.

Germer is an avid kayaker, cyclist, camper, and adventurer who lives in Dunedin, Florida.

Want More?

To continue your comeback, visit fawngermer.com to check out Fawn's online courses and coaching programs.

For speaking and coaching information:
info@fawngermer.com
(727) 467-0202

P.S. Fawn loves to hear from readers and would love to hear from you.